Mug Cakes Cookbook:

365 Days of Quick and Delectable Microwavable Cake Recipes | From Classic Favorites to Seasonal Specialties

By:
Samuel Stormwood

Table of Contents

Chapter 7 Indulgent Chocolate and Nutty Creations 72

Introduction

In the vast realm of gastronomy, there exists a culinary marvel that brings forth delight in its simplest form - the humble yet extraordinary mug cake. As you embark on this delectable journey, we invite you to explore the world of "Mug Cakes," where simplicity and creativity meet to revolutionize your approach to dessert and beyond.

In a world that often glorifies complexity, "Mug Cakes" seeks to remind us that extraordinary flavors can emerge from the simplest of ingredients. With a microwave, a few basic components, and a mug, you can conjure a dessert that rivals the most intricate of confections. But beyond their ease of preparation, mug cakes are a celebration of customization. They invite you to be the architect of your own sweet symphony.

Within these pages, you will discover not just recipes, but a passport to a world where classic and innovative flavors merge effortlessly. From rich, molten chocolate to zesty citrus, from the comforting warmth of cinnamon to the exotic allure of matcha, "Mug Cakes" is your guide to a diverse and delicious dessert landscape.

What sets this book apart is its unwavering commitment to simplicity and convenience. You'll find no complicated instructions or mysterious ingredients here. Instead, we offer you a treasure trove of single-serving wonders that can be whipped up in mere minutes, ready to satisfy your cravings, and never overstaying their welcome in the kitchen.

This book is not just about indulgence; it's about experimentation and personalization. Mug cakes are the canvas, and you are the artist. By harnessing the potential of everyday pantry staples, you can mold your dessert experience according to your preferences. With every swirl of a spoon, each dash of flavor, you create a unique masterpiece.

So, why "Mug Cakes," you may ask? The answer lies in the sheer joy that these delightful treats can bring into your life. In a world that's perpetually in motion, where time often feels like a scarce resource, mug cakes are your swift and satisfying respite. They are your go-to companions for midnight cravings, surprise guests, or simply for those moments when you need a pick-me-up.

As you peruse these pages, you'll embark on a journey that transcends the boundaries of tradition. We'll delve into not only the realm of sweet, decadent mug cakes but also their savory counterparts, expanding your culinary horizons. Mug cakes transform the ordinary into the extraordinary, making everyday ingredients dance to the tune of your cravings.

But "Mug Cakes" doesn't stop at recipes; it's a comprehensive exploration of the phenomenon of mug cakes. We'll traverse the historical origins of these single-serve delights and witness their evolution from necessity to a global culinary sensation. The journey of the mug cake is a testament to human innovation, convenience, and the relentless pursuit of deliciousness.

Now, as you stand at the threshold of the "Mug Cakes" experience, we urge you to open your heart and your kitchen to this world of simplicity, creativity, and satisfaction. Let the aroma of your favorite flavors fill your home, and the delightful tastes dance on your palate. Allow "Mug Cakes" to empower you to be the dessert artist you've always wanted to be, and do so in a fraction of the time.

We invite you to bring these recipes to life, explore their versatility, and make them your own. As you embark on this journey through the world of mug cakes, you'll discover that a simple mug can become your gateway to culinary bliss.

If you're a seasoned home cook, "Mug Cakes" offers you the tools to add a new dimension to your culinary repertoire. For those just beginning their culinary adventure, this book provides a gentle entry point, welcoming you to the world of cooking with open arms.

In the chapters that follow, you'll find inspiration, guidance, and a dash of creativity. Each recipe is designed to be not just a collection of ingredients but a canvas for your own culinary masterpiece. We encourage you to dive in, whisk, mix, and savor the wonderful world of mug cakes.

"Buy the book, implement its secrets, and unlock the door to a realm of delectable possibilities. With "Mug Cakes" in your hands, you hold the key to an array of sweet and savory experiences, each just a microwave away. The delightful world of mug cakes is ready to be explored and savored. So, let's begin our adventure together, one mug cake at a time."

Chapter 1
The Joy of Mug Cakes

- Introduction to the concept of mug cakes

Mug cakes, a delightful culinary innovation, have taken the world by storm. These miniature wonders offer an enticing blend of simplicity and indulgence. Picture a cake, traditionally requiring an array of ingredients, an oven, and your undivided attention, shrunk into a single serving. Mug cakes turn this convention on its head, making dessert preparation an effortless endeavor.

Emerging as a true emblem of modern convenience, mug cakes require nothing more than a microwave, a few readily available ingredients, and your favorite mug. The idea is as ingenious as it is practical: a dessert that can be prepared in minutes, offering a personal, delectable treat without the hassle of a traditional cake.

The history of mug cakes is an intriguing journey, born out of the need for quick and uncomplicated desserts. It's said that the concept gained popularity during the microwave oven's advent in the mid-20th century. With this new kitchen appliance, experimentation ensued, leading to the birth of the very first microwave mug cake recipes. Since then, they've continued to evolve, adapting to our ever-busier lives and our constant craving for something sweet or savory.

Mug cakes have an undeniable allure, and their charm lies in their adaptability. From rich, molten chocolate cakes to light and fruity options, mug cakes cater to a wide spectrum of tastes and occasions. These recipes are versatile, allowing for endless customization and creative twists.

As we delve deeper into the world of mug cakes, you'll discover not only the fundamental techniques for crafting the perfect mug cake but also an array of recipes that will tempt your taste buds and inspire your inner chef. So, pick up your favorite mug, gather the ingredients, and embark on a journey through the delightful universe of mug cakes

- The history and evolution of mug cakes

The origins of mug cakes can be traced back to a confluence of innovation, convenience, and culinary experimentation. While the concept of single-serving cakes had been around for centuries, it was the advent of microwave ovens in the mid-20th century that catalyzed the evolution of what we now know as mug cakes.

In the post-World War II era, the microwave oven emerged as a revolutionary kitchen appliance. Its ability to cook or heat food quickly and efficiently was nothing short of a game-changer. As people began to explore the possibilities of this new technology, it didn't take long for them to recognize its potential for simplifying the baking process.

The first iterations of microwave mug cakes were basic, often comprised of simple ingredients like flour, sugar, and milk. Enthusiastic home cooks and bakers were quick to experiment with this newfound convenience. In the early days, these experimental bakers faced a learning curve as they adjusted traditional cake recipes to suit the microwave's unique cooking properties. But their efforts laid the foundation for what would become a beloved culinary trend.

The 1980s saw the publication of early microwave recipe books that included a few mug cake recipes. These were rudimentary, often limited to vanilla or chocolate flavors. Still, they sparked interest and inspired further exploration.

As microwave technology advanced and microwave-safe cookware, including microwave-safe mugs, became more widely available, the appeal of mug cakes grew. By the turn of the 21st century, mug cake recipes had become a popular online phenomenon. Home cooks, bloggers, and food enthusiasts began sharing their inventive variations and creative flavor combinations, propelling the trend to new heights.

Mug cakes have continued to evolve, not only in terms of flavor and variety but also in their adaptability to dietary preferences. Today, you can find a wide range of recipes catering to gluten-free, vegan, keto, and other dietary needs. The creative possibilities are nearly limitless, with countless ingredients and flavors to explore.

The history of mug cakes is a testament to the human drive to innovate and simplify. What began as a convenient solution for a quick dessert has transformed into a global culinary sensation, a testament to our desire for indulgence without the fuss. Mug cakes have become a symbol of modern cooking, allowing us to savor the sweet satisfaction of a homemade cake, one mug at a time.

- The appeal of mug cakes quick, easy, and satisfying

Mug cakes have captured the hearts and taste buds of culinary enthusiasts worldwide, and it's not difficult to understand why. These charming single-serving desserts offer an irresistible combination of swiftness, simplicity, and gratification that has made them a beloved culinary trend. Let's delve into what makes mug cakes so appealing:

1. Quick and Convenient: Mug cakes are the epitome of convenience. In a world where time is often in short supply, the ability to whip up a delectable dessert in a matter of minutes is a godsend. No need to preheat an oven, no extended mixing or baking times—just swift satisfaction. The microwave, a staple in most kitchens, becomes your trusty companion in creating these little delights.

2. Minimal Mess and Cleanup: Traditional baking often involves an array of bowls, utensils, and baking pans, leading to a mountain of dirty dishes. Mug cakes, on the other hand, necessitate only a single mug and a few utensils, minimizing the post-dessert cleanup. This simplicity is especially appreciated when you're craving a sweet treat but don't want the hassle of a full-scale baking project.

3. Single-Serving Indulgence: Mug cakes offer portion control in its most delicious form. It's a personalized dessert experience, just for you. You don't have to worry about leftover cake tempting you from the kitchen counter, nor do you have to share your sweet creation if you don't want to. It's a guilt-free indulgence that allows you to enjoy a delectable treat without overindulging.

4. Endless Variety: Mug cakes are a canvas for creativity. Their simple base recipe can be customized with an array of flavors, mix-ins, and toppings. Whether you're in the mood for classic chocolate, fruity delights, or something savory, there's a mug cake recipe to suit every taste and craving. This versatility ensures that you can enjoy a unique dessert experience each time you make one.

5. Instant Gratification: There's something deeply satisfying about watching your mug cake rise and bubble in the microwave, filling your kitchen with the aroma of freshly baked goodness. It's a sensory experience that heightens anticipation and provides immediate reward, offering a moment of culinary delight amid the demands of daily life.

The appeal of mug cakes lies in their ability to deliver a delightful, homemade dessert experience in the blink of an eye. They are a testament to the beauty of simplicity in cooking, offering a delicious escape from the hustle and bustle of modern living. Whether you're a busy professional seeking a quick treat or a home cook looking for a creative outlet, mug cakes are a delightful addition to your culinary repertoire.

- What readers can expect from the book?

As you embark on the delicious journey through the pages of "Mug Cakes," we invite you to indulge your senses and creativity. This book is your gateway to a world of single-serving desserts that are as quick and easy to make as they are satisfying to savor. Here's a tantalizing sneak peek at what awaits you within these pages:

1. The Art of Mug Cakes: We'll begin by delving into the art of mug cake creation. Learn about the origins, evolution, and the allure of these delightful single-serving desserts. Discover why they've become a global culinary sensation and why they continue to captivate the hearts of food enthusiasts.

2. Essential Tools and Ingredients: Before you start creating your mug cakes, we'll guide you through the tools and ingredients you need to achieve the perfect results. From the right mug or ramekin to key components like flour, sugar, and leavening agents, we've got you covered.

3. Mastering the Basics: Get ready to roll up your sleeves as we walk you through the fundamental techniques for crafting the perfect mug cake. We'll provide you with step-by-step instructions, tips, and tricks to ensure your mug cakes turn out just the way you want them, every time.

4. Classic Dessert Mug Cakes: Indulge in a variety of classic dessert mug cake recipes that are sure to satisfy your sweet tooth. From rich and gooey chocolate creations to the comforting warmth of vanilla, these recipes will become your go-to choices for quick and delightful desserts.

5. Fruity Delights and Breakfast Mug Cakes: Experience the burst of freshness with our fruity delights, perfect for a morning pick-me-up or a light and refreshing dessert. These recipes will add a zing of flavor to your mug cake repertoire, making them suitable for any time of day.

6. Indulgent Chocolate and Nutty Creations: For the chocoholics and nut lovers among us, this chapter will be a true treat. Dive into a world of decadent chocolate and nut-infused mug cakes that will satisfy your most intense cravings.

7. Savory Mug Cakes for Quick Meals: Mug cakes aren't limited to dessert; they can also serve as quick, savory meals. We'll introduce you to an array of savory mug cake recipes that make for easy and delicious lunches, dinners, or snacks.

8. Mug Cake Hacks and Creative Twists: Elevate your mug cake game with innovative ideas and creative twists. Learn how to present your mug cakes beautifully, discover unique flavor combinations, and experiment with unusual ingredients to create memorable dessert experiences.

Throughout this book, you'll find detailed instructions, tips for success, and stunning, high-quality images to inspire your culinary adventures. Each recipe is designed to be approachable, allowing both beginners and seasoned bakers to embrace the art of mug cakes. Get ready to explore a world of flavor, convenience, and creativity as we unlock the secrets of these delightful single-serving treats. Your journey through the pages of "Mug Cakes" promises to be a mouthwatering and memorable experience.

Chapter 2
Essential Tools and Ingredients

- The basic tools you need for making mug cakes

Mug cakes are celebrated for their simplicity and speed of preparation. To create these delectable single-serving treats, you won't need an extensive collection of kitchen equipment. The charm of mug cakes lies in their ability to transform a handful of ingredients into a delightful dessert with minimal fuss. Here, we'll delve into the basic tools you need for making mug cakes, providing additional details to enhance your mug cake-making experience:

1. Microwave-Safe Mug or Ramekin: The choice of your microwave-safe container is pivotal to the success of your mug cake. Opt for a mug or ramekin that can hold approximately 1two to 1six ounces (350-47five ml) of batter. It's important to use a container that is labeled "microwave-safe" to ensure safe and even cooking. A wide, round shape is preferable, as it allows the cake to cook evenly and rise without overflowing. The beauty of mug cakes is that you can use your favorite mug, adding a personal touch to your dessert.

2. Measuring Cupful and Spoons: Accurate measurements are paramount in achieving the perfect mug cake. To ensure the right balance of ingredients, invest in a set of measuring cupful and spoons. These indispensable tools help you precisely measure items such as flour, sugar, and milk. When measuring ingredients for your mug cake, level off dry ingredients like flour and sugar with a flat edge for accuracy.

3. Mixing Utensils: To create a smooth and well-mixed batter, you'll need some basic mixing utensils. A small whisk or a fork works perfectly for this purpose. Whisks are excellent for ensuring that dry and wet ingredients are thoroughly combined, while forks can be used to achieve a similar result. The key is to blend the ingredients until there are no lumps, ensuring a deliciously consistent texture.

4. Microwave Oven: The central appliance in mug cake preparation is, of course, the microwave oven. Most standard microwaves will suffice for cooking mug cakes. However, be aware of your microwave's wattage, as it can impact cooking times. Generally, microwaving your mug cake for 1-two minutes is standard, but this may vary depending on your microwave's power. Understanding your microwave's settings and wattage can help you achieve the best results.

5. Microwave Timer: To maintain precise control over the cooking time of your mug cake, make use of your microwave's built-in timer. Familiarize yourself with how to set and adjust the timer as needed. Timing is crucial in preventing your cake from overcooking and becoming dry or undercooking, leaving it uncooked in the center. Once you've mixed your ingredients and placed the mug in the microwave, set the timer accordingly, and enjoy the anticipation of your delicious creation.

6. Heatproof Surface or Pot Holder: When your mug cake is ready, it will be hot, so it's important to have a heatproof surface or a pot holder on hand. Safeguard your hands and kitchen surfaces by placing your hot mug on a heatproof coaster, trivet, or pot holder when you remove it from the microwave. This extra layer of protection is a simple but crucial safety measure.

With these basic tools, you have everything you need to start your mug cake-making journey. The simplicity of mug cakes, combined with the minimal equipment required, makes them an ideal choice for a quick, satisfying dessert or snack. Whether you're a novice cook looking to start your culinary adventures or a seasoned chef seeking a swift and delightful treat, mug cakes provide a hassle-free and delicious solution.

- A list of essential ingredients and their roles

To master the art of creating delectable mug cakes, it's essential to understand the roles of each ingredient and how they contribute to the texture, flavor, and overall success of your miniature dessert. Here's a detailed list of these essential ingredients and their specific functions in the mug cake-making process:

1. All-Purpose Flour:

- Role: The structural foundation of your mug cake. It provides the necessary gluten to give the cake structure and stability as it rises.

2. Granulated Sugar:

- Role: Sweetens the cake, enhances flavor, and contributes to the cake's tenderness and moistness. Sugar also aids in browning.

3. Baking Powder:

- Role: A leavening agent that generates carbon dioxide gas when combined with liquid and heat. This gas production results in the rising and fluffiness of the cake.

4. Salt:

- Role: Balances sweetness, enhances overall flavor, and adds depth to the cake's taste. A pinch of salt can make a world of difference in flavor balance.

5. Milk:

- Role: Provides moisture to the batter and contributes to the cake's texture. The type of milk used can also impact the flavor and richness of the cake.

6. Cooking Oil (e.g., vegetable oil or melted butter):

- Role: Adds moisture and richness to the cake. The oil keeps the cake tender and prevents it from drying out during microwaving.

7. Egg:

- Role: Offers structure and moisture to the cake. The proteins in eggs coagulate during cooking, providing stability, while the fats contribute to a moist and tender crumb.

8. Flavor Extracts (e.g., vanilla or almond extract):

- Role: Elevates the flavor profile of the cake. These extracts add depth and richness, making your mug cake taste more like a traditional baked dessert.

9. Cocoa Powder (for chocolate mug cakes):

- Role: Provides the rich chocolate flavor and deep color in chocolate mug cakes. Unsweetened cocoa powder is commonly used for a balanced cocoa flavor.

10. Mix-Ins (e.g., chocolate chips, nuts, fruit pieces): Role: Enhances the texture of your mug cake and introduces bursts of flavor. Mix-ins provide delightful surprises with every bite.

11. Toppings (e.g., whipped cream, icing, fruit, or sprinkles): Role: Adds the final flourish to your mug cake, improving presentation and contributing to the overall taste and visual appeal.

12. Spices (e.g., cinnamon or nutmeg): Role: Elevates the flavor complexity of your cake. Spices add warmth and depth to the taste, creating a more sophisticated dessert.

13. Sweeteners (e.g., honey or maple syrup): Role: These natural sweeteners can replace granulated sugar, offering unique flavors and adding moisture to the cake.

14. Lemon or Lime Zest (for citrus-infused cakes): Role: Adds a vibrant burst of citrusy freshness, enhancing the overall flavor and aroma of your cake.

15. Cream of Tartar (for stabilizing egg whites in meringue toppings): Role: Essential for creating a stable and fluffy meringue topping in recipes like lemon meringue mug cakes. It helps maintain the structure and volume of whipped egg whites.

Understanding the intricate roles of these essential ingredients empowers you to navigate mug cake recipes with precision and creativity. Whether you're crafting a classic vanilla mug cake, indulging in a rich chocolate creation, or embarking on an exciting flavor combination, these ingredients lay the groundwork for a world of culinary possibilities. Experiment, customize, and enjoy the art of mug cake making to its fullest extent!

- Tips on selecting the right mug or ramekin

Choosing the perfect mug or ramekin is a crucial step in the journey of crafting a flawless mug cake. The right vessel can significantly impact the texture and even cooking of your dessert. Here are some valuable tips to consider when selecting the ideal mug or ramekin for your mug cakes:

1. Microwave-Safe Materials:

- Ensure that the mug or ramekin you choose is made of microwave-safe materials. Look for labels indicating "microwave-safe" or "oven-safe" to guarantee that it can withstand the heat of the microwave without cracking or releasing harmful chemicals.

2. Size Matters:

- Opt for a mug or ramekin that is the right size for your recipe. A mug with a capacity of 1two to 1six ounces (350-47five ml) is often ideal, as it allows ample room for the cake to rise without overflowing.

3. Shape and Design:

- Consider the shape of the mug or ramekin. A wide, round shape works best for even cooking and a consistent rise. Avoid tall, narrow mugs, as they can cause the cake to cook unevenly.

4. Smooth Interior:

- Look for a mug or ramekin with a smooth interior. This minimizes the chances of your cake sticking to the sides, making it easier to enjoy your creation without any leftover residue.

5. Heat-Resistant Handle:

- If you're using a mug with a handle, make sure it is heat-resistant. Some mugs may have handles that get very hot during microwaving, so be cautious to prevent burns.

6. Non-Textured Surfaces:

- Avoid mugs or ramekins with textured or embossed surfaces on the interior, as they can lead to uneven cooking and may result in pockets of overcooked or undercooked cake.

7. Material Choice:

- Ceramic and stoneware mugs are popular choices due to their even heat distribution. They retain heat well and result in a more evenly cooked mug cake. Porcelain and glass ramekins are also excellent options for achieving even cooking.

8. Light-Colored Mugs:

- Light-colored mugs or ramekins are recommended for monitoring the cake's progress during microwaving. You'll be able to see any uneven cooking or unexpected issues more clearly.

9. Multipurpose Mugs:

- Consider choosing mugs or ramekins that can serve multiple purposes. Selecting ones that you can use for coffee, tea, or other dishes in addition to mug cakes is a space-saving and practical choice.

10. Quantity and Personalization:

- Depending on your household, consider choosing mugs or ramekins that allow you to prepare multiple mug cakes at once if needed. Personalize your mug choices to reflect your style and taste.

By following these tips, you'll be well-prepared to select the right mug or ramekin for your mug cakes. Remember that your choice of vessel can impact the outcome of your dessert, so make your selection wisely to ensure a delightful, even-cooked, and visually pleasing final product.

- Understanding microwave power settings

Microwave power settings play a significant role in the successful creation of mug cakes. Different power settings can affect the cooking time, texture, and overall quality of your dessert. To ensure your mug cake turns out just the way you want it, it's crucial to understand and use microwave power settings effectively. Here's a comprehensive guide to help you navigate these settings:

1. Full Power (100% or High):

- This is the default setting for most microwave ovens. When you cook your mug cake on full power, it provides consistent and even heat, resulting in a quicker cooking time.
- Ideal for recipes that call for short cooking times (typically 1-two minutes) and a high temperature. Full power is perfect for achieving a quick and evenly baked mug cake.

2. 50-70% Power (Medium to Medium-High):

- Using lower power settings is beneficial for delicate ingredients or recipes that require a longer cooking time. It helps prevent overcooking and promotes a more even texture.
- Ideal for recipes with additional ingredients, like fruits or custards, and those with longer cooking times (2-four minutes). Lower power settings allow for gradual and thorough cooking without the risk of overheating.

3. 30% Power and Below (Low and Defrost):

- These settings are mainly used for defrosting or gently reheating food. They generate minimal heat and are not recommended for most mug cake recipes.

- They can be useful for melting ingredients like chocolate or butter before adding them to your mug cake batter. However, for actual cooking, it's best to use higher power settings.

Tips for Selecting the Right Power Setting:

1. **Check the Recipe:** Review the specific mug cake recipe you're using. It should provide guidance on the recommended power setting and cooking time. If not, a good rule of thumb is to start with full power and adjust if necessary.
2. **Experiment Gradually:** If you're unsure about the ideal power setting, it's perfectly fine to experiment. Start with a medium power setting and gradually increase or decrease it as needed for your recipe.
3. **Power Adjustment:** If your microwave allows for power adjustment, you can manually set it to your preferred level. For example, if a recipe recommends 50% power, you can select this setting to achieve more controlled cooking.
4. **Avoid Overcooking:** Keep an eye on your mug cake during cooking, especially if you're trying a new recipe or power setting. Overcooking can result in a dry and less appealing texture.
5. **Stirring:** If your recipe suggests stirring during cooking, follow the instructions to ensure even heat distribution. Stirring prevents uneven cooking and hot spots in the mug cake.
6. **Microwave Wattage:** Keep in mind that microwave wattage can vary, and this can affect cooking times. Higher-wattage microwaves may require shorter cooking times, while lower-wattage microwaves may need longer.

Understanding and effectively using microwave power settings can make a significant difference in the quality of your mug cakes. By following the recommended power settings in your recipes and making adjustments when necessary, you'll be well on your way to mastering the art of creating perfectly cooked, delectable mug cakes.

- How to customize mug cake recipes based on dietary preferences?

Mug cakes are incredibly versatile, making them a suitable choice for a variety of dietary preferences, including vegan, gluten-free, keto, and more. Here's how to customize mug cake recipes to align with specific dietary requirements:

1. Vegan Mug Cakes:

- **Replace Eggs:** Substitute eggs with plant-based alternatives like applesauce, mashed bananas, or flaxseed meal mixed with water. These ingredients act as binding agents similar to eggs.
- **Dairy-Free Milk:** Use dairy-free milk such as almond, soy, oat, or coconut milk instead

of regular milk. These alternatives work well in most recipes without compromising the taste.

- **Non-Dairy Butter or Oil:** Swap out butter with non-dairy alternatives like coconut oil, vegan butter, or olive oil. These options provide the necessary moisture and fat content.
- **Check Sweeteners:** Ensure your sweeteners, like honey, are replaced with vegan-friendly choices such as maple syrup, agave nectar, or plant-based sweeteners.

2. Gluten-Free Mug Cakes:

- **Flour Alternatives:** Use gluten-free flours like almond flour, coconut flour, rice flour, or a gluten-free flour blend. These alternatives ensure that the mug cake is safe for those with gluten sensitivities or celiac disease.
- **Gluten-Free Baking Powder:** Verify that the baking powder you use is labeled as gluten-free to prevent any contamination.

3. Keto Mug Cakes:

- **Low-Carb Sweeteners:** Replace traditional sugar with low-carb sweeteners like stevia, erythritol, or monk fruit sweetener to maintain the keto-friendly aspect of your mug cake.
- **Almond or Coconut Flour:** These low-carb flours can replace all-purpose flour to keep the carb count low.
- **Full-Fat Ingredients:** Opt for full-fat ingredients such as heavy cream, butter, or coconut cream to adhere to the high-fat, low-carb keto diet.

4. Nut-Free Mug Cakes:

- **Flour Alternatives:** Choose nut-free flours like rice flour, oat flour, or even gluten-free flour blends that do not contain almond flour or coconut flour.
- **Dairy Milk:** Use regular dairy milk or a dairy-free alternative like oat milk or soy milk if the person's nut allergy does not extend to dairy.

5. Low-Sugar Mug Cakes:

- **Natural Sweeteners:** Use natural sweeteners like honey, maple syrup, or mashed ripe fruits like bananas to reduce the added sugar content.
- **Portion Control:** Make smaller servings by reducing the sugar and sweeteners. This keeps the dessert lightly sweet while lowering overall sugar content.

6. High-Protein Mug Cakes:

- **Protein Powder:** Incorporate protein powder into your recipe to boost the protein content.

Choose a flavor that complements your mug cake, such as chocolate or vanilla.

- **Greek Yogurt:** Add Greek yogurt for extra protein and creaminess.

7. Dietary-Friendly Toppings:

- Customize your toppings to suit dietary preferences. For instance, use dairy-free whipped cream for vegan diets or low-carb berries for keto diets.

When customizing mug cake recipes to align with dietary preferences, remember that experimentation is key. It may take a few tries to get the perfect balance of ingredients and flavors, but the beauty of mug cakes is that they are forgiving and adaptable. By following the general guidelines provided for specific dietary preferences and being open to trying new ingredients, you can enjoy a delicious mug cake tailored to your dietary needs or those of your guests.

Chapter 3
Mastering the Mug Cake Basics

- The fundamental steps for making a mug cake

Making a mug cake is a quick and enjoyable process that can satisfy your sweet cravings in a matter of minutes. Here are the fundamental steps to create a basic mug cake:

Ingredients You'll Need:

- four tablespoonful all-purpose flour
- two tablespoonful granulated sugar
- one-fourth teaspoonful baking powder
- A pinch of salt
- three tablespoonful milk
- Half teaspoonful vanilla extract
- one Half tablespoonful vegetable oil (or melted butter)
- Optional mix-ins or toppings (e.g., chocolate chips, nuts, or fruit)

Equipment You'll Need:

- Microwave-safe mug or ramekin (12-1six oz/350-47five ml capacity)

- Measuring cupful and spoons
- Fork or small whisk
- Microwave oven
- Heatproof surface or pot holder (for removing the hot mug from the microwave)

Instructions:

1. Preparation:

- Start by selecting the right mug or ramekin that's microwave-safe and the appropriate size for your recipe.
- Measure out all the required ingredients and have them ready for mixing.

2. Mixing Dry Ingredients:

- In your mug, combine the all-purpose flour, granulated sugar, baking powder, and a pinch of salt. Stir these dry ingredients together until they are well combined.

3. Adding Wet Ingredients:

- Add the milk, vanilla extract, and vegetable oil (or melted butter) to the mug. Mix these wet ingredients into the dry ingredients, ensuring everything is well incorporated. Stir until you have a smooth batter with no lumps.

4. Optional Mix-Ins:

- If you want to enhance your mug cake, consider adding mix-ins such as chocolate chips, chopped nuts, or fruit pieces. Gently fold them into the batter.

5. Microwave Cooking:

- Place the mug in the microwave oven. Cook your mug cake on high (100% power) for about 1-two minutes. Cooking times may vary based on your microwave's wattage, so keep an eye on it to prevent overcooking. The cake should rise, set, and look dry on top.

6. Cooling and Serving:

- Use a heatproof surface or pot holder to remove the hot mug from the microwave carefully. Let it cool for a minute or two.
- You can enjoy your mug cake straight from the mug or gently run a knife around the edges to loosen it and then transfer it to a plate for a neater presentation.

- Add toppings like whipped cream, icing, fresh fruit, or a dusting of cocoa powder, if desired.

7. Savor Your Creation:

- Your mug cake is now ready to be savored. Grab a fork and dig in while it's warm and fresh for the best taste and texture.

Mug cakes are highly customizable, so feel free to experiment with flavors and toppings to suit your preferences. The fundamental steps for making a mug cake are easy to follow, making it a perfect treat for satisfying your dessert cravings in a flash.

- Troubleshooting common issues and mistakes

Troubleshooting Common Issues and Mistakes in Mug Cake Making:

1. Overcooking:
   - Issue: Your mug cake is dry, tough, or rubbery.
   - Solution: Reduce the cooking time or adjust the microwave power setting. Start with less time and add increments if needed to avoid overcooking. The cake should be slightly gooey when you remove it from the microwave, as it will continue to cook as it cools.
2. Undercooking:
   - Issue: The center of your mug cake is still runny or uncooked.
   - Solution: Increase the cooking time in 10-1five second intervals until the center is set. Keep in mind that it's better to slightly undercook a mug cake than to overcook it, as it will continue to cook as it cools.
3. Uneven Cooking:
   - Issue: Your mug cake is cooked on the edges but remains liquid in the center.
   - Solution: Stir the batter thoroughly before microwaving to distribute the heat more evenly. Additionally, ensure your microwave turntable is functioning correctly to help with uniform cooking.
4. Sinking or Collapsing:
   - Issue: Your mug cake deflates or collapses after cooking.
   - Solution: This can happen if you overmix the batter, causing it to lose its structure. Mix the batter just until the ingredients are combined, avoiding excessive stirring. Also, be sure your baking powder is fresh and hasn't expired, as this can affect the cake's rise.
5. Sticky Texture:
   - Issue: Your mug cake has a gummy or sticky texture.
   - Solution: This can result from overcooking or too much liquid. Adjust the cooking time, reduce the amount of liquid, or experiment with different recipes. Also, make

sure you're using the correct measurements for your ingredients.

6. Bland Flavor:
   - Issue: Your mug cake lacks flavor or tastes bland.
   - Solution: Enhance the flavor by adding extra extracts (vanilla, almond, etc.), spices (cinnamon, nutmeg), or mix-ins (chocolate chips, fruit pieces). You can also experiment with different sweeteners, like maple syrup or honey, to create a more robust taste.

7. Dry Texture:
   - Issue: Your mug cake is dry and crumbly.
   - Solution: Be careful not to overcook your mug cake, as this can lead to a dry texture. Additionally, consider adding a bit more fat, like butter or oil, to the batter to improve moisture content.

8. Taste of Baking Powder:
   - Issue: Your mug cake has a noticeable baking powder taste.
   - Solution: Ensure you're using fresh baking powder and that you've measured it accurately. Reducing the amount of baking powder slightly can also help alleviate the taste issue.

9. Mug Overflow:
   - Issue: Your mug cake overflows while cooking.
   - Solution: Use a larger mug or ramekin to allow more space for the cake to rise without spilling over. Additionally, check the wattage of your microwave, as higher-wattage microwaves may require shorter cooking times.

10. Burnt Top:
    - Issue: The top of your mug cake becomes burnt or dry during microwaving.
    - Solution: Reduce the cooking time or use a lower microwave power setting. You can also cover the mug with a microwave-safe plate to prevent the top from overcooking.

11. Excessive Mix-Ins:
    - Issue: Your mug cake is overloaded with mix-ins, making it difficult to cook evenly.
    - Solution: Be mindful of the amount of mix-ins you add to your mug cake, as excessive additions can hinder even cooking. Stick to a reasonable quantity, and consider adding some on top as a garnish after cooking.

12. Adherence to Mug:
    - Issue: Your mug cake sticks to the sides of the mug or ramekin.
    - Solution: Ensure that you grease the interior of the mug or ramekin with a small amount of oil or cooking spray before adding the batter. This will help the cake release easily after cooking.

By addressing these common issues and mistakes, you can enhance your mug cake-making skills and enjoy delicious, perfect results each time you prepare this delightful single-serving dessert.

- Tips for achieving the perfect texture and flavor

Mug cakes are all about delivering a delicious dessert in a flash, but achieving the perfect texture and flavor requires some finesse. Here are some in-depth tips to help you master the art of mug cake creation:

1. Measure Accurately:
   - Precise measurements are crucial in baking. Using measuring cupful and spoons ensures that you're adding the right amount of each ingredient. This helps maintain the perfect balance of flavors and textures in your mug cake.
2. Use Fresh Baking Powder:
   - Check the expiration date on your baking powder. Expired or old baking powder can result in a flat, less flavorful mug cake. Fresh baking powder is essential for proper leavening.
3. Don't Overmix:
   - Overmixing the batter can lead to a tough or rubbery texture. Mix the ingredients until just combined. Don't worry if there are a few lumps in the batter; they will typically disappear during cooking.
4. Flavor Enhancers:
   - Elevate your mug cake's flavor by incorporating extracts like vanilla, almond, or even citrus extracts. Spices like cinnamon, nutmeg, or even a pinch of salt can add depth and complexity to the taste. Experiment with different flavor combinations to suit your palate.
5. Sweeteners:
   - Customize the level of sweetness in your mug cake by adjusting the type and amount of sweetener used. You can opt for granulated sugar, brown sugar, honey, maple syrup, or other alternatives, depending on your dietary preferences.
6. Moisture Matters:
   - Ensure your mug cake has enough moisture to avoid dryness. Ingredients like milk, yogurt, applesauce, or fruit puree not only add moisture but also contribute to the texture. Experiment with different moisture sources to achieve the desired consistency.
7. Fat Content:
   - Fat is a key contributor to a rich and tender texture. Incorporate sources like butter, oil, or nut butters. The type of fat you choose can also influence the overall flavor, so select one that complements your chosen flavors.
8. Texture Additions:
   - To enhance texture and add delightful surprises, consider adding mix-ins like chocolate chips, chopped nuts, fruit pieces, or even mini marshmallows. Distribute these mix-ins evenly throughout the batter to ensure a balanced mix of flavors and textures.

9. Microwave Timing:
   - The cooking time and microwave power settings are critical. Pay close attention to these factors to avoid overcooking or undercooking your mug cake. The ideal result is a slightly gooey center when you remove it from the microwave.
10. Mix-Ins Distribution:
    - If you're adding mix-ins like chocolate chips or nuts, ensure they are distributed evenly throughout the batter. This ensures that every bite contains a balanced mix of flavors and textures.
11. Toppings:
    - Customize your mug cake further with complementary toppings. Whipped cream, ice cream, chocolate or caramel sauce, or a dusting of powdered sugar can enhance both the flavor and presentation of your dessert.
12. Experiment:
    - Mug cakes are versatile and forgiving. Don't be afraid to experiment with different ingredients, flavors, and combinations. The possibilities are endless, and your creativity can lead to the discovery of exciting new flavor profiles.
13. Grease the Mug:
    - To prevent your mug cake from sticking to the sides, lightly grease the interior of the mug or ramekin before adding the batter. This simple step makes it easier to remove the cake after cooking.
14. Quality Ingredients:
    - Using high-quality ingredients can elevate your mug cake. For instance, opt for real vanilla extract instead of imitation, and choose fresh, ripe fruits or premium nuts to enhance both the flavor and texture.
15. Microwave Wattage:
    - Be aware of your microwave's wattage. This can affect cooking times. Adjust your cooking time if your microwave has a higher or lower wattage than the standard model.
16. Resting Time:
    - Allow your mug cake to rest for a minute or two after microwaving. This brief resting period helps the cake set and cool slightly, improving both the texture and overall taste.

By following these comprehensive tips, you can fine-tune your mug cake-making skills and create a single-serving dessert with the perfect texture and flavor to satisfy your sweet cravings. Mug cakes are versatile and forgiving, making them an ideal canvas for culinary experimentation and creativity. Enjoy your culinary adventures!

Chapter 4
Mug Cake Hacks and Creative Twists

- Innovative ways to take your mug cakes to the next level

Mug cakes have gained popularity for their convenience and deliciousness, but if you're looking to elevate your mug cake experience, there are plenty of innovative ways to do so. These creative ideas will make your mug cakes even more impressive:

1. Layered Mug Cakes:
    - Take your mug cake to new heights by creating layers. Microwave the batter in two separate layers. After cooking the first layer, add a delicious filling like Nutella, fruit compote, or caramel. Then, top it with more batter and microwave again. This method yields a multi-textured and flavorful dessert that's as visually appealing as it is tasty.
2. Mug Cake Parfait:
    - Transform your mug cake into a parfait by layering it with yogurt or whipped cream, fresh fruit, and crumbled cookies or nuts. The layering adds depth to your mug cake with varying textures and flavors, making each spoonful a delightful surprise.
3. Mug Cake Sundae:
    - Turn your mug cake into a sundae by topping it with a scoop of ice cream, hot fudge sauce, whipped cream, and a sprinkling of colorful sprinkles or crushed nuts. The

contrast of hot and cold, along with the variety of toppings, makes it an irresistible treat.

4. Stuffed Mug Cakes:
   - Add a delightful surprise inside your mug cake by stuffing it with ingredients like a piece of chocolate, a peanut butter cupful, or a scoop of ice cream. As the cake bakes, the filling melts and creates a luscious and gooey center.

5. Mug Cake Tiramisu:
   - Soak your mug cake layers in coffee or espresso before layering them with mascarpone cheese, cocoa powder, and a generous dusting of chocolate. This mini-tiramisu takes the elegance of the classic dessert and shrinks it into a mug-sized indulgence.

6. Mug Cake Ice Cream Sandwich:
   - Slice your mug cake horizontally and use it as the "bread" for an ice cream sandwich. Add a generous scoop of your favorite ice cream between the cake layers, and roll the sides in a medley of toppings like mini chocolate chips, crushed cookies, or rainbow sprinkles.

7. Mug Cake Truffles:
   - Crumble your mug cake, combine it with a bit of frosting, and roll the mixture into small truffle-sized balls. Coat these delectable bites in melted chocolate and let them set. These mug cake truffles are perfect for gifting or indulging.

8. Mug Cake Bread Pudding:
   - Transform your mug cake into a quick bread pudding by slicing it and soaking the slices in a mixture of milk, eggs, sugar, and your favorite spices. Bake it in the oven until it's set, and savor a comforting and custardy dessert.

9. Mug Cake Milkshake:
   - Crumble your mug cake into a blender, add a scoop of ice cream, and blend it into a decadent mug cake milkshake. Top it with a dollop of whipped cream and extra cake crumbles for an indulgence that's both sippable and spoonable.

10. Mug Cake S'mores Dip:
    - Create a s'mores-inspired mug cake by topping it with mini marshmallows and broken pieces of chocolate, then briefly broil it in the oven or use a kitchen torch to brown the marshmallows. This delightful dessert mimics the classic campfire treat in a creative way.

11. Mug Cake Affogato:
    - Combine a scoop of vanilla ice cream with a freshly brewed shot of espresso or strong coffee. Pour this creamy, caffeinated concoction over your warm mug cake, creating an affogato-inspired dessert that strikes a harmonious balance between hot and cold, sweet and bitter.

12. Mug Cake Pancakes:
    - Convert your mug cake into pancake batter by thinning it with a bit of milk. Cook small portions of these mini pancakes on a griddle or stovetop, and stack them with layers of

your favorite toppings, such as fresh fruit, syrup, and whipped cream.

13. Mug Cake Waffles:
   - Similar to pancakes, you can adapt your mug cake batter into waffle batter. Cook the waffles until they're crispy and golden, then serve them with a drizzle of syrup, a dollop of whipped cream, and a handful of fresh berries for a unique twist on breakfast.

14. Mug Cake Fondue:
   - Turn your mug cake into bite-sized pieces and dip them into a warm, velvety chocolate fondue. This interactive dessert is ideal for sharing with friends or loved ones, as you create your own combination of cake and chocolate dips.

15. Mug Cake Tart:
   - Slice your mug cake horizontally and use it as the base for a mini tart. Top it with pastry cream, fresh fruit, or a drizzle of fruit compote for a gourmet presentation. This elegant touch turns your simple mug cake into a sophisticated dessert.

These innovative ideas open up a world of possibilities for taking your mug cakes to the next level. Feel free to experiment with these concepts, mix and match, and create your own signature mug cake variations. The beauty of mug cakes is their versatility and adaptability, allowing you to explore your culinary creativity and create extraordinary desserts in the blink of an eye. Enjoy the adventure of crafting these delicious single-serving treats!

- Tips for enhancing the presentation of your mug cakes

Mug cakes are not only about taste but also about the visual appeal. Elevate the presentation of your mug cakes to make them look as delightful as they taste. Here are some tips to enhance their presentation:

1. Use Attractive Mugs or Ramekins:
   - Choose mugs or ramekins with eye-catching designs or colors that complement your mug cake. Aesthetically pleasing containers add an extra layer of visual appeal.

2. Layered Toppings:
   - Create layers of toppings on your mug cake. Start with a dollop of whipped cream or ice cream, then add a drizzle of sauce (like chocolate or caramel), and finish with a sprinkle of nuts, colorful sprinkles, or fresh fruit.

3. Garnish with Fresh Fruit:
   - Top your mug cake with fresh, colorful fruit like berries, slices of kiwi, or a fan of strawberry. Fresh fruit not only adds a pop of color but also a touch of freshness.

4. Dusting of Powdered Sugar or Cocoa:
   - A light dusting of powdered sugar or cocoa powder over your mug cake can make it look more elegant. Use a fine sieve or sifter to achieve an even and professional appearance.

5. Arrange in a Sundae Glass:
   - Serve your mug cake in a clear sundae glass or dessert bowl to showcase the layers and toppings. This presentation makes your mug cake look like a sophisticated dessert.
6. Decorative Plates:
   - Choose decorative or vintage-style plates to serve your mug cakes. The right plate can elevate the overall presentation.
7. Drizzle or Swirl Sauces:
   - Drizzle a sauce in an artistic pattern on top of your mug cake. Use a spoon or a squeeze bottle to create swirls, zigzags, or a delicate lattice.
8. Edible Flowers:
   - Edible flowers like pansies, violets, or nasturtiums can add a touch of elegance to your mug cake presentation. Ensure the flowers are safe to eat and pesticide-free.
9. Sprinkle of Nuts or Seeds:
   - A sprinkle of chopped nuts, like almonds, pistachios, or hazelnuts, can provide both visual interest and a delightful crunch to your mug cake.
10. Whipped Cream Rosettes:
    - Pipe whipped cream onto your mug cake in the shape of rosettes using a pastry bag and a star tip. This adds a lovely and professional touch.
11. Chocolate Shavings or Curls:
    - Use a vegetable peeler to create delicate chocolate shavings or curls and arrange them artistically on top of your mug cake.
12. Mini Umbrella or Cocktail Accessories:
    - For a fun twist, insert a mini umbrella or cocktail accessories (like tiny drink umbrellas) into your mug cake. This adds a playful and whimsical element to the presentation.
13. Rimmed Mug:
    - Dip the rim of your mug in melted chocolate and then in colorful sprinkles or crushed cookies for a fun and interactive presentation.
14. Customized Toppers:
    - Create customized toppers with edible images, personalized messages, or thematic decorations that match the occasion or your personal style.
15. Serving Boards or Trays:
    - Serve your mug cakes on wooden boards or elegant trays. This creates a more refined and stylish presentation.
16. Stencils or Templates:
    - Use stencils or templates to dust powdered sugar, cocoa, or spices in intricate designs on your mug cake.
17. Color Coordination:
    - Pay attention to color coordination between your mug cake, toppings, and presentation. Harmonious color schemes can make your dessert more visually appealing.

18. Minimalistic Elegance:
    - Sometimes, less is more. Embrace minimalism by focusing on the quality of ingredients and the overall simplicity of presentation.
19. Photography Presentation:
    - If you're sharing your mug cake creations on social media, consider investing in photography props and backgrounds to make your photos visually stunning.
20. Serving Platters with Mini Utensils:
    - Place your mug cake on a decorative serving platter and offer mini dessert forks or spoons. This presentation adds a touch of sophistication.

Enhancing the presentation of your mug cakes not only makes them more inviting but also allows you to showcase your creativity and attention to detail. Experiment with these tips to create visually stunning mug cakes that are a feast for the eyes as well as the taste buds.

- Unique flavor combinations and creative toppings

One of the joys of making mug cakes is experimenting with unusual flavor combinations and innovative toppings. Here are some unique ideas to inspire your creativity:

Flavor Combinations:

1. **Orange Creamsicle:** Infuse your mug cake batter with orange zest and a touch of vanilla extract, and top it with a dollop of whipped cream and a sprinkle of orange zest.
2. **Banana Nut Bread:** Add mashed ripe banana to your batter and mix in chopped walnuts. Top with a drizzle of honey and a sprinkle of cinnamon.
3. **Chai Spice:** Mix ground cinnamon, cardamom, and a pinch of black tea leaves into your batter. Top with a chai-spiced glaze made from powdered sugar and milk.
4. **Lavender Lemon:** Add a hint of dried culinary lavender to your batter, and top your mug cake with a delicate lemon glaze and a few fresh lavender blossoms.
5. **Maple Pecan:** Incorporate maple syrup and chopped pecans into your batter. Drizzle with more maple syrup and sprinkle with additional pecans.
6. **Pistachio Rose:** Use ground pistachios in your batter and flavor it with a drop of rose water. Top with a rose-scented whipped cream and crushed pistachios.
7. **Mango Tango:** Mix in diced mango pieces to your batter and serve your mug cake with a scoop of mango sorbet on top.
8. **Mojito Mug Cake:** Infuse your cake with fresh lime zest and a hint of mint extract. Top it with a lime glaze and a sprig of fresh mint.
9. **Black Forest Delight:** Incorporate chopped cherries and cocoa powder into your batter. After cooking, add a dollop of whipped cream, a cherry on top, and some chocolate shavings.

10. **Matcha Red Bean:** Blend matcha green tea powder into your batter and top it with sweetened red bean paste, known as "anko."
11. **Savory Herb Mug Cake:** Experiment with savory flavors by adding chopped fresh herbs like rosemary, thyme, and chives to your batter. Top with a dollop of sour cream or crème fraîche.

Creative Toppings:

12. **Candied Bacon:** Sprinkle your mug cake with crumbled candied bacon for a sweet and salty contrast.
13. **Crunchy Cereal:** Top your cake with a scoop of your favorite cereal, like granola, cornflakes, or cinnamon toast crunch.
14. **Savory Cheese:** For a savory twist, add a spoonful of shredded cheese like cheddar or parmesan, and broil it for a crispy, cheesy topping.
15. **Edible Flowers:** Garnish your mug cake with edible flowers like pansies, violets, or marigold petals for a touch of elegance.
16. **Toasted Coconut:** Sprinkle toasted coconut flakes over your cake for a tropical and crunchy topping.
17. **Candied Nuts:** Top your mug cake with candied nuts, like pecans or almonds, for an indulgent texture and flavor.
18. **Cookie Crumbles:** Add crushed cookies or biscotti on top of your cake for an extra layer of texture and a delightful surprise.
19. **Popcorn Magic:** Sprinkle popcorn over your cake for a playful and unexpected topping. Drizzle with caramel or chocolate for added decadence.
20. **Sesame Seeds:** Toasted sesame seeds add a delightful nutty crunch to your mug cake. Consider pairing them with flavors like tahini or honey for an exciting twist.
21. **Spicy Kick:** Grate a small amount of chili chocolate or sprinkle cayenne pepper on top of your chocolate mug cake for a spicy and sweet flavor combination.
22. **Fruit Salsa:** Create a quick fruit salsa to serve with your cake. Dice fresh fruit like strawberries, kiwi, and pineapple and toss with a drizzle of honey and a squeeze of lime juice.
23. **Mini Marshmallow Madness:** For a whimsical touch, cover your mug cake with mini marshmallows and briefly toast them under a broiler or with a kitchen torch.
24. **Elegant Cocoa Dusting:** Use a lace doily or stencil to create intricate cocoa powder designs on top of your mug cake for a visually stunning presentation.
25. **Colorful Candy Gems:** Decorate your cake with colorful, edible gems or candy pearls for a dazzling and playful appearance.

These unique flavor combinations and creative toppings offer endless opportunities to make your mug cakes stand out. Let your taste buds and imagination guide you as you explore these delightful and unexpected combinations.

- Incorporating unusual ingredients and culinary influences

Mug cakes offer a canvas for culinary experimentation, and incorporating unusual ingredients and culinary influences can lead to surprising and delectable results. Here are some innovative ideas to inspire your creative journey:

Unusual Ingredients:

1. **Sour Cream:** Add a dollop of sour cream to your batter for extra moisture and a slight tang, resulting in a tender and flavorful cake.
2. **Balsamic Reduction:** Drizzle a balsamic reduction over your finished mug cake for a unique sweet and tangy twist.
3. **Avocado:** Mash ripe avocado into your batter to create a creamy and moist texture. The avocado's natural sweetness pairs well with chocolate flavors.
4. **Soy Sauce:** A dash of soy sauce can deepen the umami flavor of a chocolate or caramel mug cake.
5. **Turmeric:** Incorporate ground turmeric into your batter for an earthy and slightly spicy mug cake. It pairs well with honey or ginger.
6. **Sake:** Replace some of the liquid in your batter with sake for a subtle alcoholic kick and a complex flavor profile.
7. **Tahini:** Blend tahini, a sesame paste, into your batter for a nutty and slightly savory profile. It pairs wonderfully with honey or halva.
8. **Miso Paste:** A small amount of miso paste can add depth and saltiness to your sweet mug cake, creating a unique contrast.
9. **Cayenne Pepper:** A pinch of cayenne pepper can give your chocolate mug cake a delightful, subtle heat that enhances the richness of the chocolate.
10. **Lavender Blossoms:** Incorporate dried culinary lavender blossoms into your batter for a fragrant, floral note that pairs well with lemon or white chocolate.

Culinary Influences:

11. **Indian Spices:** Infuse your batter with a blend of Indian spices like cardamom, cinnamon, and cloves for a chai-inspired mug cake.
12. **Japanese Matcha:** Incorporate matcha green tea powder into your batter and finish with a dusting of matcha or a matcha glaze for a unique Asian twist.
13. **Middle Eastern Flavors:** Use ingredients like rosewater, pistachios, and orange blossom water for a Middle Eastern-inspired mug cake with a delightful exotic flair.
14. **Mexican Mole:** Add cocoa powder, cinnamon, and a hint of chili to your batter for a mug cake reminiscent of the complex flavors of Mexican mole.

15. **Mediterranean Flavors:** Create a Mediterranean-inspired mug cake with ingredients like chopped dates, figs, or a drizzle of honey for a taste of the Mediterranean's sweetness.
16. **Thai Coconut:** Mix in coconut milk and a touch of lemongrass to your batter, and top it with a creamy coconut glaze for a Thai-inspired delight.
17. **Greek Baklava:** Incorporate chopped nuts, honey, and a hint of cinnamon into your batter for a mug cake that captures the essence of Greek baklava.
18. **French Lavender:** Use dried lavender flowers and a touch of lemon zest for a French-inspired, aromatic mug cake.
19. **Moroccan Spice:** Combine exotic spices like cumin, coriander, and ginger into your batter for a mug cake with a Moroccan flair.
20. **Caribbean Coconut Rum:** Add shredded coconut and a splash of rum to your batter for a Caribbean-inspired delight. Top with a rum glaze for an extra kick.
21. **Italian Tiramisu:** Create a tiramisu-inspired mug cake by infusing your cake with coffee and mascarpone cheese. Top with cocoa powder and a drizzle of coffee liqueur.
22. **Peruvian Chocolate:** Use Peruvian chocolate or cocoa powder, which often has unique fruity and floral notes, to create a distinctive chocolate mug cake.
23. **Scandinavian Lingonberry:** Incorporate lingonberry jam or sauce into your batter for a Scandinavian-inspired mug cake. Top with a dollop of whipped cream.
24. **South American Churro:** Blend cinnamon and sugar into your batter and top it with a churro-inspired caramel sauce and a sprinkle of cinnamon sugar.
25. **Chinese Five-Spice:** Create a Chinese-inspired mug cake by adding Chinese five-spice powder to your batter for a complex flavor profile with notes of anise, cloves, and cinnamon.

Experiment with these unusual ingredients and culinary influences to create mug cakes that transport your taste buds around the world and offer unexpected and delightful flavors. Embrace the adventure of culinary fusion and discover new taste sensations.

- Expert advice on creating special occasion mug cakes

Mug cakes can be the perfect sweet treat for any special occasion, from birthdays to anniversaries, or just a cozy evening in. Here's some expert advice to ensure your special occasion mug cakes are a hit:

1. Choose the Right Flavors:
   - Consider the guest of honor's favorite flavors when crafting your special occasion mug cake. Whether it's chocolate, fruit, or a unique combination, tailor the cake to their preferences.
2. Layered or Stacked Creations:
   - Special occasions call for elevated presentations. Create layered mug cakes by baking

multiple layers separately and stacking them with layers of frosting, whipped cream, or fruit fillings in between.

3. Customized Toppers:
   - Personalize your mug cakes with custom toppers. These could be edible images, fondant decorations, or even a short, heartfelt message that's tailored to the occasion.

4. Use Themed Mugs:
   - Select mugs or ramekins that match the theme of the occasion. You can find mugs with birthday designs, anniversary messages, or seasonal motifs to enhance the festive atmosphere.

5. Special Icing and Frosting:
   - Consider using a special icing or frosting. Whether it's a rich chocolate ganache, a creamy cream cheese frosting, or a citrus-infused glaze, unique frosting choices can elevate your mug cake.

6. Edible Flowers and Gold Leaf:
   - For a touch of elegance, use edible flowers like pansies, violet petals, or even edible gold leaf to decorate your mug cakes. These additions are perfect for weddings, bridal showers, and anniversaries.

7. Chocolate Dipped Edges:
   - Dip the rim of your mug in melted chocolate and then roll it in crushed nuts, sprinkles, or edible glitter for an elegant and delectable presentation.

8. Whipped Cream Rosettes:
   - Pipe whipped cream into rosettes or other decorative shapes using a pastry bag and a star tip. These serve as a beautiful and delicious topping for your mug cake.

9. Flavor-Infused Syrups:
   - Create a selection of flavor-infused syrups like raspberry, lavender, or coffee to drizzle over your mug cakes. These add unique flavor profiles to your creations.

10. Sculpted Garnishes:
    - Craft sculpted garnishes from chocolate or marzipan to decorate your mug cakes. These can be as simple as hearts for Valentine's Day or more intricate designs for weddings.

11. Creative Layering:
    - Experiment with creative layering by adding a layer of fruit compote, mousse, or even a mini scoop of ice cream between the cake layers for a surprising burst of flavor and texture.

12. Savory Mug Cakes:
    - Don't limit yourself to sweet mug cakes. For special occasions, you can create savory options with ingredients like cheese, herbs, and even smoked salmon or caviar.

13. Personalized Messages:
    - Customize your mug cakes with personal messages or greetings written in edible ink or with melted chocolate. It's a thoughtful touch for birthdays and anniversaries.

14. Fancy Plating:
   - Serve your mug cakes on elegant dessert plates or platters. Garnish the plate with artistic drizzles, fruit coulis, or a dusting of powdered sugar for a polished look.
15. Candlelit Presentation:
   - For romantic occasions, serve your mug cakes with a lit candle in a secure holder for a cozy and intimate ambiance.
16. Photo Mug Cakes:
   - Create a photo mug cake by printing an edible image on a layer of fondant and placing it on top of your mug cake.
17. Combining Special Occasions:
   - When multiple special occasions overlap, such as a birthday and an anniversary, create a mug cake that celebrates both. Customize it with symbols or themes relevant to both occasions.
18. Cocktail-Inspired Mug Cakes:
   - Infuse your mug cakes with the flavors of popular cocktails like margaritas, piña coladas, or mojitos for a unique and adult-friendly treat.
19. Creative Crumbles:
   - Top your mug cake with inventive crumbles like candied bacon, pretzel pieces, or cookie dough for a playful and memorable twist.
20. Dessert Shooters:
   - Transform your mug cake into a dessert shooter by layering it with cake, frosting, and toppings in a shot glass for an elegant and miniature treat.

Remember that the key to creating special occasion mug cakes is personalization and attention to detail. Consider the preferences and dietary restrictions of your guests, and tailor your creations to match the ambiance and theme of the celebration. Whether it's a birthday, anniversary, or a spontaneous romantic evening, your mug cakes can be a delightful centerpiece for any special occasion.

Chapter 5
Classic Dessert Mug Cakes

1.   Chocolate Lava Mug Cake:

Ingredients:

- two tablespoonful all-purpose flour
- two tablespoonful granulated sugar
- two tablespoonful unsweetened cocoa powder
- one-fourth teaspoonful baking powder
- a pinch of salt
- two tablespoonful milk
- one tablespoonful vegetable oil
- one-fourth teaspoonful vanilla extract
- one square (10g) of dark chocolate

Instructions:

1. In a microwave-safe mug, whisk together the flour, sugar, cocoa powder, baking powder, and salt.
2. Add the milk, vegetable oil, and vanilla extract. Stir until well combined.

3. Place the chocolate square in the center of the batter.
4. Microwave on high for 45-60 seconds until the cake rises and the center is still slightly gooey.
5. Let it cool for a minute and enjoy.

Duration: 1-two minutes

Nutrients per portion (Approximate):

- Caloric content: 320
- Amino content: 5g
- Carb content: 44g
- Fatty acid: 15g
- Fiber content: 4g

2.   Vanilla Mug Cake:

Ingredients:

- four tablespoonful all-purpose flour
- three tablespoonful granulated sugar
- one-fourth teaspoonful baking powder
- a pinch of salt
- three tablespoonful milk
- two tablespoonful vegetable oil
- Half teaspoonful vanilla extract

Instructions:

1. In a microwave-safe mug, whisk together the flour, sugar, baking powder, and salt.
2. Add the milk, vegetable oil, and vanilla extract. Stir until well combined.
3. Microwave on high for 1-one and a half minutes until the cake is set.
4. Let it cool for a minute before serving.

Duration: One and a half-two minutes

Nutrients per portion (Approximate):

- Caloric content: 450
- Amino content: 5g
- Carb content: 58g

- Fatty acid: 21g
- Fiber content: 1g

3. Strawberry Shortcake Mug Cake:

Ingredients:

- four tablespoonful all-purpose flour
- two tablespoonful granulated sugar
- one-fourth teaspoonful baking powder
- a pinch of salt
- three tablespoonful milk
- two tablespoonful vegetable oil
- Half teaspoonful vanilla extract
- one-fourth cupful fresh strawberries, chopped
- Whipped cream (for topping)

Instructions:

1. In a microwave-safe mug, whisk together the flour, sugar, baking powder, and salt.
2. Add the milk, vegetable oil, and vanilla extract. Stir until well combined.
3. Gently fold in the chopped strawberries.
4. Microwave on high for 1-one and a half minutes until the cake is set.
5. Top with whipped cream before serving.

Duration: One and a half-two minutes

Nutrients per portion (Approximate):

- Caloric content: 480
- Amino content: 5g
- Carb content: 66g
- Fatty acid: 23g
- Fiber content: 2g

4. Molten Caramel Mug Cake:

Ingredients:

- two tablespoonful all-purpose flour
- three tablespoonful granulated sugar

- one tablespoonful unsweetened cocoa powder
- one-fourth teaspoonful baking powder
- a pinch of salt
- two tablespoonful milk
- one tablespoonful vegetable oil
- one-fourth teaspoonful vanilla extract
- one caramel candy (e.g., Rolo)

Instructions:

1. In a microwave-safe mug, whisk together the flour, sugar, cocoa powder, baking powder, and salt.
2. Add the milk, vegetable oil, and vanilla extract. Stir until well combined.
3. Place the caramel candy in the center of the batter.
4. Microwave on high for 45-60 seconds until the cake rises and the caramel inside is gooey.
5. Let it cool for a minute and enjoy.

Duration: 1-two minutes

Nutrients per portion (Approximate):

- Caloric content: 350
- Amino content: 3g
- Carb content: 54g
- Fatty acid: 16g
- Fiber content: 2g

5.   Classic Chocolate Chip Mug Cookie:

Ingredients:

- two tablespoonful all-purpose flour
- one Half tablespoonful granulated sugar
- one-fourth teaspoonful baking powder
- a pinch of salt
- one tablespoonful butter, melted
- one-fourth teaspoonful vanilla extract
- one tablespoonful chocolate chips

Instructions:

1. In a microwave-safe mug, whisk together the flour, sugar, baking powder, and salt.
2. Add the melted butter and vanilla extract. Stir until well combined.
3. Gently fold in the chocolate chips.
4. Microwave on high for 45-60 seconds until the cookie is set but still soft.
5. Let it cool for a minute and enjoy.

Duration: 1-two minutes

Nutrients per portion (Approximate):

- Caloric content: 370
- Amino content: 3g
- Carb content: 48g
- Fatty acid: 19g
- Fiber content: 1g

6.   Red Velvet Mug Cake:

Ingredients:

- four tablespoonful all-purpose flour
- two Half tablespoonful granulated sugar
- one-fourth teaspoonful baking powder
- one tablespoonful unsweetened cocoa powder
- a pinch of salt
- three tablespoonful buttermilk
- one Half tablespoonful vegetable oil
- one-fourth teaspoonful vanilla extract
- one-fourth teaspoonful red food coloring

Instructions:

1. In a microwave-safe mug, whisk together the flour, sugar, baking powder, cocoa powder, and salt.
2. Add the buttermilk, vegetable oil, vanilla extract, and red food coloring. Stir until well combined.
3. Microwave on high for One and a half-two minutes until the cake is set.
4. Let it cool for a minute before serving.

Duration: One and a half-two minutes

Nutrients per portion (Approximate):

- Caloric content: 450
- Amino content: 5g
- Carb content: 60g
- Fatty acid: 21g
- Fiber content: 2g

7.   Lemon Blueberry Mug Cake:

Ingredients:

- four tablespoonful all-purpose flour
- three tablespoonful granulated sugar
- one-fourth teaspoonful baking powder
- a pinch of salt
- three tablespoonful milk
- two tablespoonful vegetable oil
- one-fourth teaspoonful lemon zest
- one-fourth teaspoonful lemon juice
- one-fourth cupful fresh blueberries

Instructions:

1. In a microwave-safe mug, whisk together the flour, sugar, baking powder, and salt.
2. Add the milk, vegetable oil, lemon zest, and lemon juice. Stir until well combined.
3. Gently fold in the fresh blueberries.
4. Microwave on high for One and a half-two minutes until the cake is set.
5. Let it cool for a minute before serving.

Duration: One and a half-two minutes

Nutrients per portion (Approximate):

- Caloric content: 420
- Amino content: 4g
- Carb content: 55g
- Fatty acid: 21g
- Fiber content: 2g

8. Banana Nut Mug Cake:

Ingredients:

- three tablespoonful all-purpose flour
- two tablespoonful granulated sugar
- one-fourth teaspoonful baking powder
- a pinch of salt
- two tablespoonful milk
- one Half tablespoonful vegetable oil
- Half ripe banana, mashed
- one tablespoonful chopped nuts (e.g., walnuts or pecans)

Instructions:

1. In a microwave-safe mug, whisk together the flour, sugar, baking powder, and salt.
2. Add the milk, vegetable oil, and mashed banana. Stir until well combined.
3. Gently fold in the chopped nuts.
4. Microwave on high for 1-one and a half minutes until the cake is set.
5. Let it cool for a minute before serving.

Duration: 1-one and a half minutes

Nutrients per portion (Approximate):

- Caloric content: 370
- Amino content: 3g
- Carb content: 51g
- Fatty acid: 18g
- Fiber content: 2g

9. Cinnamon Roll Mug Cake:

Ingredients:

- four tablespoonful all-purpose flour
- two Half tablespoonful granulated sugar
- one-fourth teaspoonful baking powder
- a pinch of salt
- three tablespoonful milk
- one Half tablespoonful vegetable oil

- one-fourth teaspoonful vanilla extract
- Half teaspoonful ground cinnamon
- one tablespoonful butter, melted
- Half tablespoonful brown sugar
- Cream cheese glaze (optional)

Instructions:

1. In a microwave-safe mug, whisk together the flour, sugar, baking powder, and salt.
2. Add the milk, vegetable oil, vanilla extract, and ground cinnamon. Stir until well combined.
3. In a separate bowl, combine the melted butter and brown sugar.
4. Pour the cinnamon-sugar mixture over the cake batter in the mug.
5. Microwave on high for One and a half-two minutes until the cake is set.
6. Drizzle with cream cheese glaze, if desired, before serving.

Duration: One and a half-two minutes

Nutrients per portion (Approximate):

- Caloric content: 430
- Amino content: 4g
- Carb content: 57g
- Fatty acid: 20g
- Fiber content: 2g

10.   Peanut Butter Chocolate Mug Cake:

Ingredients:

- three tablespoonful all-purpose flour
- three tablespoonful granulated sugar
- one Half tablespoonful unsweetened cocoa powder
- one-fourth teaspoonful baking powder
- a pinch of salt
- two tablespoonful milk
- one Half tablespoonful creamy peanut butter
- one-fourth teaspoonful vanilla extract
- one tablespoonful chocolate chips

Instructions:

1. In a microwave-safe mug, whisk together the flour, sugar, cocoa powder, baking powder, and salt.
2. Add the milk, peanut butter, and vanilla extract. Stir until well combined.
3. Gently fold in the chocolate chips.
4. Microwave on high for 1-one and a half minutes until the cake is set.
5. Let it cool for a minute before serving.

Duration: 1-one and a half minutes

Nutrients per portion (Approximate):

- Caloric content: 380
- Amino content: 6g
- Carb content: 51g
- Fatty acid: 17g
- Fiber content: 3g

11.   Cookies and Cream Mug Cake:

Ingredients:

- four tablespoonful all-purpose flour
- three tablespoonful granulated sugar
- one-fourth teaspoonful baking powder
- a pinch of salt
- three tablespoonful milk
- one Half tablespoonful vegetable oil
- two chocolate sandwich cookies (e.g., Oreos), crushed

Instructions:

1. In a microwave-safe mug, whisk together the flour, sugar, baking powder, and salt.
2. Add the milk and vegetable oil. Stir until well combined.
3. Gently fold in the crushed chocolate sandwich cookies.
4. Microwave on high for One and a half-two minutes until the cake is set.
5. Let it cool for a minute before serving.

Duration: One and a half-two minutes

Nutrients per portion (Approximate):

- Caloric content: 420
- Amino content: 4g
- Carb content: 55g
- Fatty acid: 21g
- Fiber content: 2g

12.   Apple Spice Mug Cake:

Ingredients:

- four tablespoonful all-purpose flour
- three tablespoonful granulated sugar
- one-fourth teaspoonful baking powder
- a pinch of salt
- three tablespoonful milk
- two tablespoonful unsweetened applesauce
- one-fourth teaspoonful ground cinnamon
- a pinch of ground nutmeg

Instructions:

1. In a microwave-safe mug, whisk together the flour, sugar, baking powder, and salt.
2. Add the milk, unsweetened applesauce, ground cinnamon, and ground nutmeg. Stir until well combined.
3. Microwave on high for One and a half-two minutes until the cake is set.
4. Let it cool for a minute before serving.

Duration: One and a half-two minutes

Nutrients per portion (Approximate):

- Caloric content: 320
- Amino content: 4g
- Carb content: 68g
- Fatty acid: 2g
- Fiber content: 2g

13.   Carrot Cake Mug Cake:

Ingredients:

- four tablespoonful all-purpose flour
- three tablespoonful granulated sugar
- one-fourth teaspoonful baking powder
- a pinch of salt
- three tablespoonful milk
- two tablespoonful vegetable oil
- one-fourth teaspoonful vanilla extract
- one-fourth cupful grated carrots
- one tablespoonful chopped walnuts (optional)
- Cream cheese frosting (for topping, optional)

Instructions:

1. In a microwave-safe mug, whisk together the flour, sugar, baking powder, and salt.
2. Add the milk, vegetable oil, and vanilla extract. Stir until well combined.
3. Gently fold in the grated carrots and chopped walnuts, if using.
4. Microwave on high for One and a half-two minutes until the cake is set.
5. Top with cream cheese frosting, if desired, before serving.

Duration: One and a half-two minutes

Nutrients per portion (Approximate):

- Caloric content: 410
- Amino content: 5g
- Carb content: 56g
- Fatty acid: 20g
- Fiber content: 2g

14.   Mint Chocolate Mug Cake:

Ingredients:

- four tablespoonful all-purpose flour
- three tablespoonful granulated sugar
- one-fourth teaspoonful baking powder
- a pinch of salt

- three tablespoonful milk
- two tablespoonful vegetable oil
- one-fourth teaspoonful peppermint extract
- one tablespoonful unsweetened cocoa powder
- one tablespoonful chocolate chips
- Green food coloring (optional)

Instructions:

1. In a microwave-safe mug, whisk together the flour, sugar, baking powder, and salt.
2. Add the milk, vegetable oil, peppermint extract, and unsweetened cocoa powder. Stir until well combined.
3. Gently fold in the chocolate chips.
4. If desired, add a drop of green food coloring to achieve a minty color.
5. Microwave on high for One and a half-two minutes until the cake is set.
6. Let it cool for a minute before serving.

Duration: One and a half-two minutes

Nutrients per portion (Approximate):

- Caloric content: 440
- Amino content: 4g
- Carb content: 57g
- Fatty acid: 22g
- Fiber content: 2g

15.   Pumpkin Pie Mug Cake:

Ingredients:

- four tablespoonful all-purpose flour
- three tablespoonful granulated sugar
- one-fourth teaspoonful baking powder
- a pinch of salt
- three tablespoonful canned pumpkin puree
- two tablespoonful milk
- one Half tablespoonful vegetable oil
- one-fourth teaspoonful ground cinnamon
- a pinch of ground nutmeg
- Whipped cream (for topping)

50

Instructions:

1. In a microwave-safe mug, whisk together the flour, sugar, baking powder, and salt.
2. Add the canned pumpkin puree, milk, vegetable oil, ground cinnamon, and ground nutmeg. Stir until well combined.
3. Microwave on high for One and a half-two minutes until the cake is set.
4. Top with whipped cream before serving.

Duration: One and a half-two minutes

Nutrients per portion (Approximate):

- Caloric content: 380
- Amino content: 4g
- Carb content: 56g
- Fatty acid: 18g
- Fiber content: 2g

16. Coffee Cake Mug Cake:

Ingredients:

- four tablespoonful all-purpose flour
- two Half tablespoonful granulated sugar
- one-fourth teaspoonful baking powder
- a pinch of salt
- three tablespoonful milk
- two tablespoonful vegetable oil
- Half teaspoonful ground cinnamon
- Half tablespoonful brown sugar
- Half tablespoonful butter, melted
- Powdered sugar (for dusting, optional)

Instructions:

1. In a microwave-safe mug, whisk together the flour, sugar, baking powder, and salt.
2. Add the milk, vegetable oil, and ground cinnamon. Stir until well combined.
3. In a separate bowl, combine the melted butter, brown sugar, and a pinch of cinnamon.
4. Pour the butter-sugar mixture over the cake batter in the mug.
5. Microwave on high for One and a half-two minutes until the cake is set.
6. Dust with powdered sugar, if desired, before serving.

Duration: One and a half-two minutes

Nutrients per portion (Approximate):

- Caloric content: 450
- Amino content: 3g
- Carb content: 60g
- Fatty acid: 21g
- Fiber content: 2g

17.   S'mores Mug Cake:

Ingredients:

- four tablespoonful all-purpose flour
- three tablespoonful granulated sugar
- one-fourth teaspoonful baking powder
- a pinch of salt
- three tablespoonful milk
- two tablespoonful vegetable oil
- one tablespoonful unsweetened cocoa powder
- two tablespoonful mini marshmallows
- two graham cracker squares, crushed
- one tablespoonful chocolate chips

Instructions:

1. In a microwave-safe mug, whisk together the flour, sugar, baking powder, and salt.
2. Add the milk, vegetable oil, and unsweetened cocoa powder. Stir until well combined.
3. Gently fold in the mini marshmallows, crushed graham cracker squares, and chocolate chips.
4. Microwave on high for One and a half-two minutes until the cake is set.
5. Let it cool for a minute before serving.

Duration: One and a half-two minutes

Nutrients per portion (Approximate):

- Caloric content: 440
- Amino content: 3g
- Carb content: 68g

- Fatty acid: 19g
- Fiber content: 2g

18. Tiramisu Mug Cake:

Ingredients:

- four tablespoonful all-purpose flour
- three tablespoonful granulated sugar
- one-fourth teaspoonful baking powder
- a pinch of salt
- three tablespoonful milk
- two tablespoonful brewed espresso or strong coffee
- Half teaspoonful unsweetened cocoa powder
- Half tablespoonful mascarpone cheese
- Half tablespoonful coffee liqueur (optional)
- Cocoa powder (for dusting, optional)

Instructions:

1. In a microwave-safe mug, whisk together the flour, sugar, baking powder, and salt.
2. Add the milk, brewed espresso, and unsweetened cocoa powder. Stir until well combined.
3. Microwave on high for One and a half-two minutes until the cake is set.
4. Top with a dollop of mascarpone cheese and a drizzle of coffee liqueur, if desired.
5. Dust with cocoa powder, if desired, before serving.

Duration: One and a half-two minutes

Nutrients per portion (Approximate):

- Caloric content: 380
- Amino content: 4g
- Carb content: 58g
- Fatty acid: 14g
- Fiber content: 2g

19. Raspberry White Chocolate Mug Cake:

Ingredients:

- four tablespoonful all-purpose flour

- three tablespoonful granulated sugar
- one-fourth teaspoonful baking powder
- a pinch of salt
- three tablespoonful milk
- two tablespoonful vegetable oil
- one-fourth teaspoonful almond extract
- two tablespoonful fresh raspberries
- one tablespoonful white chocolate chips

Instructions:

1. In a microwave-safe mug, whisk together the flour, sugar, baking powder, and salt.
2. Add the milk, vegetable oil, and almond extract. Stir until well combined.
3. Gently fold in the fresh raspberries and white chocolate chips.
4. Microwave on high for One and a half-two minutes until the cake is set.
5. Let it cool for a minute before serving.

Duration: One and a half-two minutes

Nutrients per portion (Approximate):

- Caloric content: 410
- Amino content: 3g
- Carb content: 56g
- Fatty acid: 20g
- Fiber content: 2g

20.   Black Forest Mug Cake:

Ingredients:

- four tablespoonful all-purpose flour
- three tablespoonful granulated sugar
- one-fourth teaspoonful baking powder
- a pinch of salt
- three tablespoonful milk
- two tablespoonful vegetable oil
- one-fourth teaspoonful almond extract
- one-fourth cupful canned dark sweet cherries, drained
- Whipped cream (for topping)
- Chocolate shavings (for garnish, optional)

Instructions:

1. In a microwave-safe mug, whisk together the flour, sugar, baking powder, and salt.
2. Add the milk, vegetable oil, and almond extract. Stir until well combined.
3. Gently fold in the dark sweet cherries.
4. Microwave on high for One and a half-two minutes until the cake is set.
5. Top with whipped cream and chocolate shavings, if desired, before serving.

Duration: One and a half-two minutes

Nutrients per portion (Approximate):

- Caloric content: 430
- Amino content: 3g
- Carb content: 58g
- Fatty acid: 20g
- Fiber content: 2g

Chapter 6
Fruity Delights and Breakfast Mug Cakes

21.   Blueberry Muffin Mug Cake:

Ingredients:

- four tablespoonful all-purpose flour
- three tablespoonful granulated sugar
- one-fourth teaspoonful baking powder
- a pinch of salt
- three tablespoonful milk
- two tablespoonful vegetable oil
- one-fourth teaspoonful vanilla extract
- one-fourth cupful fresh blueberries

Instructions:

1. In a microwave-safe mug, whisk together the flour, sugar, baking powder, and salt.

2. Add the milk, vegetable oil, and vanilla extract. Stir until well combined.
3. Gently fold in the fresh blueberries.
4. Microwave on high for One and a half-two minutes until the cake is set.
5. Let it cool for a minute before serving.

Duration: One and a half-two minutes

Nutrients per portion (Approximate):

- Caloric content: 400
- Amino content: 4g
- Carb content: 58g
- Fatty acid: 19g
- Fiber content: 2g

22.   Banana Nut Bread Mug Cake:

Ingredients:

- four tablespoonful all-purpose flour
- three tablespoonful granulated sugar
- one-fourth teaspoonful baking powder
- a pinch of salt
- three tablespoonful milk
- two tablespoonful vegetable oil
- Half ripe banana, mashed
- one tablespoonful chopped walnuts

Instructions:

1. In a microwave-safe mug, whisk together the flour, sugar, baking powder, and salt.
2. Add the milk, vegetable oil, and mashed banana. Stir until well combined.
3. Gently fold in the chopped walnuts.
4. Microwave on high for One and a half-two minutes until the cake is set.
5. Let it cool for a minute before serving.

Duration: One and a half-two minutes

Nutrients per portion (Approximate):

- Caloric content: 410

- Amino content: 4g
- Carb content: 56g
- Fatty acid: 19g
- Fiber content: 2g

23.   Lemon Poppy Seed Mug Cake:

Ingredients:

- four tablespoonful all-purpose flour
- three tablespoonful granulated sugar
- one-fourth teaspoonful baking powder
- a pinch of salt
- three tablespoonful milk
- two tablespoonful vegetable oil
- Half teaspoonful lemon zest
- Half teaspoonful poppy seeds
- Half teaspoonful lemon juice

Instructions:

1. In a microwave-safe mug, whisk together the flour, sugar, baking powder, and salt.
2. Add the milk, vegetable oil, lemon zest, poppy seeds, and lemon juice. Stir until well combined.
3. Microwave on high for One and a half-two minutes until the cake is set.
4. Let it cool for a minute before serving.

Duration: One and a half-two minutes

Nutrients per portion (Approximate):

- Caloric content: 420
- Amino content: 4g
- Carb content: 58g
- Fatty acid: 20g
- Fiber content: 2g

24. Strawberry Pancake Mug Cake:

Ingredients:

- four tablespoonful all-purpose flour
- two tablespoonful granulated sugar
- one-fourth teaspoonful baking powder
- a pinch of salt
- three tablespoonful milk
- one tablespoonful vegetable oil
- one-fourth teaspoonful vanilla extract
- two strawberries, diced
- Maple syrup (for topping)

Instructions:

1. In a microwave-safe mug, whisk together the flour, sugar, baking powder, and salt.
2. Add the milk, vegetable oil, and vanilla extract. Stir until well combined.
3. Gently fold in the diced strawberries.
4. Microwave on high for One and a half-two minutes until the cake is set.
5. Drizzle with maple syrup before serving.

Duration: One and a half-two minutes

Nutrients per portion (Approximate):

- Caloric content: 380
- Amino content: 4g
- Carb content: 60g
- Fatty acid: 14g
- Fiber content: 2g

25. Peach Cobbler Mug Cake:

Ingredients:

- four tablespoonful all-purpose flour
- three tablespoonful granulated sugar
- one-fourth teaspoonful baking powder
- a pinch of salt
- three tablespoonful milk

- two tablespoonful vegetable oil
- Half cupful canned peaches, drained and diced
- one-fourth teaspoonful ground cinnamon

Instructions:

1. In a microwave-safe mug, whisk together the flour, sugar, baking powder, and salt.
2. Add the milk, vegetable oil, and ground cinnamon. Stir until well combined.
3. Gently fold in the diced peaches.
4. Microwave on high for One and a half-two minutes until the cake is set.
5. Let it cool for a minute before serving.

Duration: One and a half-two minutes

Nutrients per portion (Approximate):

- Caloric content: 370
- Amino content: 3g
- Carb content: 58g
- Fatty acid: 16g
- Fiber content: 2g

26. Raspberry Almond Mug Cake:

Ingredients:

- four tablespoonful almond flour
- three tablespoonful granulated sugar
- one-fourth teaspoonful baking powder
- a pinch of salt
- three tablespoonful milk
- two tablespoonful vegetable oil
- one-fourth teaspoonful almond extract
- one-fourth cupful fresh raspberries
- Sliced almonds (for topping)

Instructions:

1. In a microwave-safe mug, whisk together the almond flour, sugar, baking powder, and salt.
2. Add the milk, vegetable oil, and almond extract. Stir until well combined.
3. Gently fold in the fresh raspberries.

4. Microwave on high for One and a half-two minutes until the cake is set.
5. Top with sliced almonds before serving.

Duration: One and a half-two minutes

Nutrients per portion (Approximate):

- Caloric content: 360
- Amino content: 4g
- Carb content: 46g
- Fatty acid: 20g
- Fiber content: 4g

27.   Mixed Berry Oatmeal Mug Cake:

Ingredients:

- four tablespoonful rolled oats
- three tablespoonful granulated sugar
- one-fourth teaspoonful baking powder
- a pinch of salt
- three tablespoonful milk
- two tablespoonful mixed berries (e.g., blueberries, strawberries, and raspberries)
- one-fourth teaspoonful vanilla extract

Instructions:

1. In a microwave-safe mug, whisk together the rolled oats, sugar, baking powder, and salt.
2. Add the milk, mixed berries, and vanilla extract. Stir until well combined.
3. Microwave on high for One and a half-two minutes until the cake is set.
4. Let it cool for a minute before serving.

Duration: One and a half-two minutes

Nutrients per portion (Approximate):

- Caloric content: 380
- Amino content: 4g
- Carb content: 70g
- Fatty acid: 5g
- Fiber content: 6g

28.   Pineapple Upside-Down Mug Cake:

Ingredients:

- four tablespoonful all-purpose flour
- three tablespoonful granulated sugar
- one-fourth teaspoonful baking powder
- a pinch of salt
- three tablespoonful milk
- two tablespoonful vegetable oil
- one-fourth cupful canned pineapple slices, drained
- Maraschino cherry (for topping)

Instructions:

1. In a microwave-safe mug, whisk together the flour, sugar, baking powder, and salt.
2. Add the milk, vegetable oil, and pineapple slices. Stir until well combined.
3. Microwave on high for One and a half-two minutes until the cake is set.
4. Top with a maraschino cherry before serving.

Duration: One and a half-two minutes

Nutrients per portion (Approximate):

- Caloric content: 400
- Amino content: 3g
- Carb content: 57g
- Fatty acid: 18g
- Fiber content: 2g

29.   Mango Coconut Mug Cake:

Ingredients:

- four tablespoonful all-purpose flour
- three tablespoonful granulated sugar
- one-fourth teaspoonful baking powder
- a pinch of salt
- three tablespoonful coconut milk
- two tablespoonful mango puree
- one-fourth teaspoonful vanilla extract

- Shredded coconut (for topping, optional)

Instructions:

1. In a microwave-safe mug, whisk together the flour, sugar, baking powder, and salt.
2. Add the coconut milk, mango puree, and vanilla extract. Stir until well combined.
3. Microwave on high for One and a half-two minutes until the cake is set.
4. Top with shredded coconut, if desired, before serving.

Duration: One and a half-two minutes

Nutrients per portion (Approximate):

- Caloric content: 380
- Amino content: 3g
- Carb content: 62g
- Fatty acid: 13g
- Fiber content: 2g

30.   Peanut Butter and Banana Breakfast Mug Cake:

Ingredients:

- four tablespoonful rolled oats
- three tablespoonful granulated sugar
- one-fourth teaspoonful baking powder
- a pinch of salt
- three tablespoonful milk
- two tablespoonful creamy peanut butter
- Half ripe banana, mashed

Instructions:

1. In a microwave-safe mug, whisk together the rolled oats, sugar, baking powder, and salt.
2. Add the milk, peanut butter, and mashed banana. Stir until well combined.
3. Microwave on high for One and a half-two minutes until the cake is set.
4. Let it cool for a minute before serving.

Duration: One and a half-two minutes

Nutrients per portion (Approximate):

- Caloric content: 420
- Amino content: 6g
- Carb content: 63g
- Fatty acid: 16g
- Fiber content: 5g

31. Raspberry Lemon Cheesecake Mug Cake:

Ingredients:

- four tablespoonful all-purpose flour
- three tablespoonful granulated sugar
- one-fourth teaspoonful baking powder
- a pinch of salt
- three tablespoonful milk
- two tablespoonful cream cheese, softened
- one-fourth teaspoonful lemon zest
- one-fourth cupful fresh raspberries

Instructions:

1. In a microwave-safe mug, whisk together the flour, sugar, baking powder, and salt.
2. Add the milk, softened cream cheese, and lemon zest. Stir until well combined.
3. Gently fold in the fresh raspberries.
4. Microwave on high for One and a half-two minutes until the cake is set.
5. Let it cool for a minute before serving.

Duration: One and a half-two minutes

Nutrients per portion (Approximate):

- Caloric content: 400
- Amino content: 5g
- Carb content: 56g
- Fatty acid: 18g
- Fiber content: 3g

32. Chai Spice Mug Cake:

Ingredients:

- four tablespoonful all-purpose flour
- three tablespoonful granulated sugar
- one-fourth teaspoonful baking powder
- a pinch of salt
- three tablespoonful milk
- one tablespoonful vegetable oil
- one-fourth teaspoonful ground cinnamon
- one-fourth teaspoonful ground cardamom
- one-fourth teaspoonful ground ginger
- one-fourth teaspoonful ground cloves
- Whipped cream (for topping)

Instructions:

1. In a microwave-safe mug, whisk together the flour, sugar, baking powder, and salt.
2. Add the milk, vegetable oil, and all the spices. Stir until well combined.
3. Microwave on high for One and a half-two minutes until the cake is set.
4. Top with a dollop of whipped cream before serving.

Duration: One and a half-two minutes

Nutrients per portion (Approximate):

- Caloric content: 370
- Amino content: 4g
- Carb content: 62g
- Fatty acid: 12g
- Fiber content: 2g

33. Pear and Caramel Mug Cake:

Ingredients:

- four tablespoonful all-purpose flour
- three tablespoonful granulated sugar
- one-fourth teaspoonful baking powder
- a pinch of salt

- three tablespoonful milk
- two tablespoonful diced ripe pear
- one tablespoonful caramel sauce

Instructions:

1. In a microwave-safe mug, whisk together the flour, sugar, baking powder, and salt.
2. Add the milk, diced pear, and caramel sauce. Stir until well combined.
3. Microwave on high for One and a half-two minutes until the cake is set.
4. Let it cool for a minute before serving.

Duration: One and a half-two minutes

Nutrients per portion (Approximate):

- Caloric content: 360
- Amino content: 3g
- Carb content: 74g
- Fatty acid: 2g
- Fiber content: 3g

34.   Cranberry Orange Mug Cake:

Ingredients:

- four tablespoonful all-purpose flour
- three tablespoonful granulated sugar
- one-fourth teaspoonful baking powder
- a pinch of salt
- three tablespoonful milk
- two tablespoonful dried cranberries
- one-fourth teaspoonful orange zest
- one-fourth teaspoonful orange extract

Instructions:

1. In a microwave-safe mug, whisk together the flour, sugar, baking powder, and salt.
2. Add the milk, dried cranberries, orange zest, and orange extract. Stir until well combined.
3. Microwave on high for One and a half-two minutes until the cake is set.
4. Let it cool for a minute before serving.

Duration: One and a half-two minutes

Nutrients per portion (Approximate):

- Caloric content: 380
- Amino content: 3g
- Carb content: 78g
- Fatty acid: 2g
- Fiber content: 2g

35.   Cinnamon Apple Mug Cake:

Ingredients:

- four tablespoonful all-purpose flour
- three tablespoonful granulated sugar
- one-fourth teaspoonful baking powder
- a pinch of salt
- three tablespoonful milk
- two tablespoonful diced apple
- one-fourth teaspoonful ground cinnamon

Instructions:

1. In a microwave-safe mug, whisk together the flour, sugar, baking powder, and salt.
2. Add the milk, diced apple, and ground cinnamon. Stir until well combined.
3. Microwave on high for One and a half-two minutes until the cake is set.
4. Let it cool for a minute before serving.

Duration: One and a half-two minutes

Nutrients per portion (Approximate):

- Caloric content: 370
- Amino content: 3g
- Carb content: 79g
- Fatty acid: 2g
- Fiber content: 3g

36.   Cherry Almond Mug Cake:

Ingredients:

- four tablespoonful all-purpose flour
- three tablespoonful granulated sugar
- one-fourth teaspoonful baking powder
- a pinch of salt
- three tablespoonful milk
- two tablespoonful chopped cherries (fresh or frozen)
- one-fourth teaspoonful almond extract
- Sliced almonds (for topping)

Instructions:

1. In a microwave-safe mug, whisk together the flour, sugar, baking powder, and salt.
2. Add the milk, chopped cherries, and almond extract. Stir until well combined.
3. Microwave on high for One and a half-two minutes until the cake is set.
4. Top with sliced almonds before serving.

Duration: One and a half-two minutes

Nutrients per portion (Approximate):

- Caloric content: 390
- Amino content: 4g
- Carb content: 72g
- Fatty acid: 8g
- Fiber content: 2g

37.   Fig and Honey Mug Cake:

Ingredients:

- four tablespoonful all-purpose flour
- three tablespoonful granulated sugar
- one-fourth teaspoonful baking powder
- a pinch of salt
- three tablespoonful milk
- two tablespoonful dried figs, chopped
- Half tablespoonful honey

Instructions:

1. In a microwave-safe mug, whisk together the flour, sugar, baking powder, and salt.
2. Add the milk, chopped dried figs, and honey. Stir until well combined.
3. Microwave on high for One and a half-two minutes until the cake is set.
4. Let it cool for a minute before serving.

Duration: One and a half-two minutes

Nutrients per portion (Approximate):

- Caloric content: 370
- Amino content: 3g
- Carb content: 82g
- Fatty acid: 2g
- Fiber content: 3g

38. Pineapple Coconut Mug Cake:

Ingredients:

- four tablespoonful all-purpose flour
- three tablespoonful granulated sugar
- one-fourth teaspoonful baking powder
- a pinch of salt
- three tablespoonful coconut milk
- two tablespoonful crushed pineapple, drained
- Half tablespoonful shredded coconut

Instructions:

1. In a microwave-safe mug, whisk together the flour, sugar, baking powder, and salt.
2. Add the coconut milk, crushed pineapple, and shredded coconut. Stir until well combined.
3. Microwave on high for One and a half-two minutes until the cake is set.
4. Let it cool for a minute before serving.

Duration: One and a half-two minutes

Nutrients per portion (Approximate):

- Caloric content: 380

- Amino content: 3g
- Carb content: 80g
- Fatty acid: 4g
- Fiber content: 2g

39. Maple Pecan Mug Cake:

Ingredients:

- four tablespoonful all-purpose flour
- three tablespoonful granulated sugar
- one-fourth teaspoonful baking powder
- a pinch of salt
- three tablespoonful milk
- Half tablespoonful maple syrup
- Half tablespoonful chopped pecans

Instructions:

1. In a microwave-safe mug, whisk together the flour, sugar, baking powder, and salt.
2. Add the milk, maple syrup, and chopped pecans. Stir until well combined.
3. Microwave on high for One and a half-two minutes until the cake is set.
4. Let it cool for a minute before serving.

Duration: One and a half-two minutes

Nutrients per portion (Approximate):

- Caloric content: 380
- Amino content: 3g
- Carb content: 73g
- Fatty acid: 6g
- Fiber content: 2g

40. Banana Split Mug Cake:

Ingredients:

- four tablespoonful all-purpose flour
- three tablespoonful granulated sugar
- one-fourth teaspoonful baking powder

- a pinch of salt
- three tablespoonful milk
- Half ripe banana, mashed
- Half tablespoonful chocolate chips
- Half tablespoonful chopped strawberries
- Whipped cream (for topping)
- Maraschino cherry (for topping)

Instructions:

1. In a microwave-safe mug, whisk together the flour, sugar, baking powder, and salt.
2. Add the milk, mashed banana, and chocolate chips. Stir until well combined.
3. Microwave on high for One and a half-two minutes until the cake is set.
4. Top with chopped strawberries, whipped cream, and a maraschino cherry before serving.

Duration: One and a half-two minutes

Nutrients per portion (Approximate):

- Caloric content: 420
- Amino content: 4g
- Carb content: 86g
- Fatty acid: 7g
- Fiber content: 4g

Chapter 7
Indulgent Chocolate and Nutty Creations

41.   Triple Chocolate Mug Cake:

Ingredients:

- four tablespoonful all-purpose flour
- three tablespoonful granulated sugar
- one-fourth teaspoonful baking powder
- a pinch of salt
- three tablespoonful milk
- two tablespoonful unsweetened cocoa powder
- one tablespoonful semi-sweet chocolate chips
- one tablespoonful white chocolate chips
- one tablespoonful milk chocolate chips

Instructions:

1. In a microwave-safe mug, whisk together the flour, sugar, baking powder, and salt.
2. Add the milk, unsweetened cocoa powder, and all three types of chocolate chips. Stir until well combined.

3. Microwave on high for One and a half-two minutes until the cake is set.
4. Let it cool for a minute before serving.

Duration: One and a half-two minutes

Nutrients per portion (Approximate):

- Caloric content: 430
- Amino content: 5g
- Carb content: 70g
- Fatty acid: 15g
- Fiber content: 3g

42.   Hazelnut Chocolate Mug Cake:

Ingredients:

- four tablespoonful all-purpose flour
- three tablespoonful granulated sugar
- one-fourth teaspoonful baking powder
- a pinch of salt
- three tablespoonful milk
- two tablespoonful unsweetened cocoa powder
- one tablespoonful hazelnut spread (like Nutella)
- one tablespoonful chopped hazelnuts

Instructions:

1. In a microwave-safe mug, whisk together the flour, sugar, baking powder, and salt.
2. Add the milk, unsweetened cocoa powder, and hazelnut spread. Stir until well combined.
3. Gently fold in the chopped hazelnuts.
4. Microwave on high for One and a half-two minutes until the cake is set.
5. Let it cool for a minute before serving.

Duration: One and a half-two minutes

Nutrients per portion (Approximate):

- Caloric content: 410
- Amino content: 5g
- Carb content: 70g

- Fatty acid: 14g
- Fiber content: 3g

43.   Peanut Butter Chocolate Chip Mug Cake:

Ingredients:

- four tablespoonful all-purpose flour
- three tablespoonful granulated sugar
- one-fourth teaspoonful baking powder
- a pinch of salt
- three tablespoonful milk
- two tablespoonful creamy peanut butter
- one tablespoonful chocolate chips

Instructions:

1. In a microwave-safe mug, whisk together the flour, sugar, baking powder, and salt.
2. Add the milk, creamy peanut butter, and chocolate chips. Stir until well combined.
3. Microwave on high for One and a half-two minutes until the cake is set.
4. Let it cool for a minute before serving.

Duration: One and a half-two minutes

Nutrients per portion (Approximate):

- Caloric content: 400
- Amino content: 6g
- Carb content: 63g
- Fatty acid: 13g
- Fiber content: 3g

44.   Rocky Road Mug Cake:

Ingredients:

- four tablespoonful all-purpose flour
- three tablespoonful granulated sugar
- one-fourth teaspoonful baking powder
- a pinch of salt
- three tablespoonful milk

- two tablespoonful mini marshmallows
- one tablespoonful chopped almonds
- one tablespoonful chocolate chips

Instructions:

1. In a microwave-safe mug, whisk together the flour, sugar, baking powder, and salt.
2. Add the milk, mini marshmallows, chopped almonds, and chocolate chips. Stir until well combined.
3. Microwave on high for One and a half-two minutes until the cake is set.
4. Let it cool for a minute before serving.

Duration: One and a half-two minutes

Nutrients per portion (Approximate):

- Caloric content: 440
- Amino content: 4g
- Carb content: 68g
- Fatty acid: 19g
- Fiber content: 2g

45.   Dark Chocolate Raspberry Mug Cake:

Ingredients:

- four tablespoonful all-purpose flour
- three tablespoonful granulated sugar
- one-fourth teaspoonful baking powder
- a pinch of salt
- three tablespoonful milk
- two tablespoonful dark chocolate chips
- one-fourth cupful fresh raspberries

Instructions:

1. In a microwave-safe mug, whisk together the flour, sugar, baking powder, and salt.
2. Add the milk and dark chocolate chips. Stir until well combined.
3. Gently fold in the fresh raspberries.
4. Microwave on high for One and a half-two minutes until the cake is set.
5. Let it cool for a minute before serving.

Duration: One and a half-two minutes

Nutrients per portion (Approximate):

- Caloric content: 400
- Amino content: 4g
- Carb content: 66g
- Fatty acid: 16g
- Fiber content: 3g

46.   White Chocolate Macadamia Nut Mug Cake:

Ingredients:

- four tablespoonful all-purpose flour
- three tablespoonful granulated sugar
- one-fourth teaspoonful baking powder
- a pinch of salt
- three tablespoonful milk
- two tablespoonful white chocolate chips
- one tablespoonful chopped macadamia nuts

Instructions:

1. In a microwave-safe mug, whisk together the flour, sugar, baking powder, and salt.
2. Add the milk and white chocolate chips. Stir until well combined.
3. Gently fold in the chopped macadamia nuts.
4. Microwave on high for One and a half-two minutes until the cake is set.
5. Let it cool for a minute before serving.

Duration: One and a half-two minutes

Nutrients per portion (Approximate):

- Caloric content: 420
- Amino content: 5g
- Carb content: 70g
- Fatty acid: 16g
- Fiber content: 2g

47.   Almond Joy Mug Cake:

Ingredients:

- four tablespoonful all-purpose flour
- three tablespoonful granulated sugar
- one-fourth teaspoonful baking powder
- a pinch of salt
- three tablespoonful milk
- one tablespoonful shredded coconut
- one tablespoonful chocolate chips
- one tablespoonful chopped almonds

Instructions:

1. In a microwave-safe mug, whisk together the flour, sugar, baking powder, and salt.
2. Add the milk, shredded coconut, chocolate chips, and chopped almonds. Stir until well combined.
3. Microwave on high for One and a half-two minutes until the cake is set.
4. Let it cool for a minute before serving.

Duration: One and a half-two minutes

Nutrients per portion (Approximate):

- Caloric content: 410
- Amino content: 5g
- Carb content: 67g
- Fatty acid: 15g
- Fiber content: 2g

48.   Chocolate Banana Nut Mug Cake:

Ingredients:

- four tablespoonful all-purpose flour
- three tablespoonful granulated sugar
- one-fourth teaspoonful baking powder
- a pinch of salt
- three tablespoonful milk
- two tablespoonful unsweetened cocoa powder

- Half ripe banana, mashed
- one tablespoonful chopped walnuts

Instructions:

1. In a microwave-safe mug, whisk together the flour, sugar, baking powder, and salt.
2. Add the milk, unsweetened cocoa powder, and mashed banana. Stir until well combined.
3. Gently fold in the chopped walnuts.
4. Microwave on high for One and a half-two minutes until the cake is set.
5. Let it cool for a minute before serving.

Duration: One and a half-two minutes

Nutrients per portion (Approximate):

- Caloric content: 420
- Amino content: 5g
- Carb content: 71g
- Fatty acid: 14g
- Fiber content: 4g

49.   Mint Chocolate Mug Cake:

Ingredients:

- four tablespoonful all-purpose flour
- three tablespoonful granulated sugar
- one-fourth teaspoonful baking powder
- a pinch of salt
- three tablespoonful milk
- one-fourth teaspoonful peppermint extract
- one tablespoonful chocolate chips
- Whipped cream (for topping)

Instructions:

1. In a microwave-safe mug, whisk together the flour, sugar, baking powder, and salt.
2. Add the milk, peppermint extract, and chocolate chips. Stir until well combined.
3. Microwave on high for One and a half-two minutes until the cake is set.
4. Top with a dollop of whipped cream before serving.

Duration: One and a half-two minutes

Nutrients per portion (Approximate):

- Caloric content: 400
- Amino content: 4g
- Carb content: 66g
- Fatty acid: 14g
- Fiber content: 2g

50.   Chocolate Espresso Mug Cake:

Ingredients:

- four tablespoonful all-purpose flour
- three tablespoonful granulated sugar
- one-fourth teaspoonful baking powder
- a pinch of salt
- three tablespoonful milk
- two tablespoonful unsweetened cocoa powder
- Half teaspoonful instant espresso powder

Instructions:

1. In a microwave-safe mug, whisk together the flour, sugar, baking powder, and salt.
2. Add the milk, unsweetened cocoa powder, and instant espresso powder. Stir until well combined.
3. Microwave on high for One and a half-two minutes until the cake is set.
4. Let it cool for a minute before serving.

Duration: One and a half-two minutes

Nutrients per portion (Approximate):

- Caloric content: 390
- Amino content: 4g
- Carb content: 76g
- Fatty acid: 12g
- Fiber content: 3g

51.   Marshmallow Mug Cake:

Ingredients:

- four tablespoonful all-purpose flour
- three tablespoonful graham cracker crumbs
- three tablespoonful granulated sugar
- one-fourth teaspoonful baking powder
- a pinch of salt
- three tablespoonful milk
- one tablespoonful unsweetened cocoa powder
- one tablespoonful chocolate chips
- one tablespoonful mini marshmallows

Instructions:

1. In a microwave-safe mug, whisk together the flour, graham cracker crumbs, sugar, baking powder, and salt.
2. Add the milk, unsweetened cocoa powder, chocolate chips, and mini marshmallows. Stir until well combined.
3. Microwave on high for One and a half-two minutes until the cake is set.
4. Let it cool for a minute before serving.

Duration: One and a half-two minutes

Nutrients per portion (Approximate):

- Caloric content: 430
- Amino content: 5g
- Carb content: 80g
- Fatty acid: 11g
- Fiber content: 3g

52.   Turtle Pecan Mug Cake:

Ingredients:

- four tablespoonful all-purpose flour
- three tablespoonful granulated sugar
- one-fourth teaspoonful baking powder
- a pinch of salt

80

- three tablespoonful milk
- one tablespoonful caramel sauce
- one tablespoonful chopped pecans
- one tablespoonful chocolate chips

Instructions:

1. In a microwave-safe mug, whisk together the flour, sugar, baking powder, and salt.
2. Add the milk, caramel sauce, chopped pecans, and chocolate chips. Stir until well combined.
3. Microwave on high for One and a half-two minutes until the cake is set.
4. Let it cool for a minute before serving.

Duration: One and a half-two minutes

Nutrients per portion (Approximate):

- Caloric content: 410
- Amino content: 4g
- Carb content: 74g
- Fatty acid: 12g
- Fiber content: 2g

53. Double Chocolate Hazelnut Mug Cake:

Ingredients:

- four tablespoonful all-purpose flour
- three tablespoonful granulated sugar
- one-fourth teaspoonful baking powder
- a pinch of salt
- three tablespoonful milk
- two tablespoonful unsweetened cocoa powder
- one tablespoonful hazelnut spread (like Nutella)
- one tablespoonful chocolate chips

Instructions:

1. In a microwave-safe mug, whisk together the flour, sugar, baking powder, and salt.
2. Add the milk, unsweetened cocoa powder, hazelnut spread, and chocolate chips. Stir until well combined.

3. Microwave on high for One and a half-two minutes until the cake is set.
4. Let it cool for a minute before serving.

Duration: One and a half-two minutes

Nutrients per portion (Approximate):

- Caloric content: 420
- Amino content: 6g
- Carb content: 69g
- Fatty acid: 14g
- Fiber content: 3g

54.   Mint Chocolate Chip Mug Cake:

Ingredients:

- four tablespoonful all-purpose flour
- three tablespoonful granulated sugar
- one-fourth teaspoonful baking powder
- a pinch of salt
- three tablespoonful milk
- one-fourth teaspoonful peppermint extract
- one tablespoonful chocolate chips
- one tablespoonful chopped fresh mint leaves

Instructions:

1. In a microwave-safe mug, whisk together the flour, sugar, baking powder, and salt.
2. Add the milk, peppermint extract, chocolate chips, and chopped fresh mint leaves. Stir until well combined.
3. Microwave on high for One and a half-two minutes until the cake is set.
4. Let it cool for a minute before serving.

Duration: One and a half-two minutes

Nutrients per portion (Approximate):

- Caloric content: 410
- Amino content: 4g
- Carb content: 76g

- Fatty acid: 10g
- Fiber content: 3g

55. Chocolate Almond Mug Cake:

Ingredients:

- four tablespoonful all-purpose flour
- three tablespoonful granulated sugar
- one-fourth teaspoonful baking powder
- a pinch of salt
- three tablespoonful milk
- two tablespoonful unsweetened cocoa powder
- one tablespoonful almond butter
- one tablespoonful chopped almonds

Instructions:

1. In a microwave-safe mug, whisk together the flour, sugar, baking powder, and salt.
2. Add the milk, unsweetened cocoa powder, almond butter, and chopped almonds. Stir until well combined.
3. Microwave on high for One and a half-two minutes until the cake is set.
4. Let it cool for a minute before serving.

Duration: One and a half-two minutes

Nutrients per portion (Approximate):

- Caloric content: 400
- Amino content: 6g
- Carb content: 70g
- Fatty acid: 14g
- Fiber content: 3g

56. Chocolate Peanut Butter Cupful Mug Cake:

Ingredients:

- four tablespoonful all-purpose flour
- three tablespoonful granulated sugar
- one-fourth teaspoonful baking powder

- a pinch of salt
- three tablespoonful milk
- two tablespoonful unsweetened cocoa powder
- one tablespoonful creamy peanut butter
- one tablespoonful chocolate chips

Instructions:

1. In a microwave-safe mug, whisk together the flour, sugar, baking powder, and salt.
2. Add the milk, unsweetened cocoa powder, creamy peanut butter, and chocolate chips. Stir until well combined.
3. Microwave on high for One and a half-two minutes until the cake is set.
4. Let it cool for a minute before serving.

Duration: One and a half-two minutes

Nutrients per portion (Approximate):

- Caloric content: 410
- Amino content: 6g
- Carb content: 70g
- Fatty acid: 14g
- Fiber content: 3g

57. Nutella and Banana Mug Cake:

Ingredients:

- four tablespoonful all-purpose flour
- three tablespoonful granulated sugar
- one-fourth teaspoonful baking powder
- a pinch of salt
- three tablespoonful milk
- two tablespoonful Nutella
- Half ripe banana, mashed

Instructions:

1. In a microwave-safe mug, whisk together the flour, sugar, baking powder, and salt.
2. Add the milk, Nutella, and mashed banana. Stir until well combined.
3. Microwave on high for One and a half-two minutes until the cake is set.

4. Let it cool for a minute before serving.

Duration: One and a half-two minutes

Nutrients per portion (Approximate):

- Caloric content: 420
- Amino content: 5g
- Carb content: 71g
- Fatty acid: 14g
- Fiber content: 3g

58. Chocolate Coconut Almond Joy Mug Cake:

Ingredients:

- four tablespoonful all-purpose flour
- three tablespoonful granulated sugar
- one-fourth teaspoonful baking powder
- a pinch of salt
- three tablespoonful milk
- two tablespoonful shredded coconut
- one tablespoonful chopped almonds
- one tablespoonful chocolate chips

Instructions:

1. In a microwave-safe mug, whisk together the flour, sugar, baking powder, and salt.
2. Add the milk, shredded coconut, chopped almonds, and chocolate chips. Stir until well combined.
3. Microwave on high for One and a half-two minutes until the cake is set.
4. Let it cool for a minute before serving.

Duration: One and a half-two minutes

Nutrients per portion (Approximate):

- Caloric content: 410
- Amino content: 4g
- Carb content: 76g
- Fatty acid: 12g

- Fiber content: 2g

59.   Mocha Almond Fudge Mug Cake:

Ingredients:

- four tablespoonful all-purpose flour
- three tablespoonful granulated sugar
- one-fourth teaspoonful baking powder
- a pinch of salt
- three tablespoonful milk
- two tablespoonful unsweetened cocoa powder
- Half teaspoonful instant coffee granules
- one tablespoonful chopped almonds

Instructions:

1. In a microwave-safe mug, whisk together the flour, sugar, baking powder, and salt.
2. Add the milk, unsweetened cocoa powder, instant coffee granules, and chopped almonds. Stir until well combined.
3. Microwave on high for One and a half-two minutes until the cake is set.
4. Let it cool for a minute before serving.

Duration: One and a half-two minutes

Nutrients per portion (Approximate):

- Caloric content: 400
- Amino content: 6g
- Carb content: 70g
- Fatty acid: 14g
- Fiber content: 3g

60.   Dark Chocolate Pistachio Mug Cake:

Ingredients:

- four tablespoonful all-purpose flour
- three tablespoonful granulated sugar
- one-fourth teaspoonful baking powder
- a pinch of salt

- three tablespoonful milk
- two tablespoonful dark chocolate chips
- one tablespoonful chopped pistachios

Instructions:

1. In a microwave-safe mug, whisk together the flour, sugar, baking powder, and salt.
2. Add the milk, dark chocolate chips, and chopped pistachios. Stir until well combined.
3. Microwave on high for One and a half-two minutes until the cake is set.
4. Let it cool for a minute before serving.

Duration: One and a half-two minutes

Nutrients per portion (Approximate):

- Caloric content: 410
- Amino content: 5g
- Carb content: 70g
- Fatty acid: 14g
- Fiber content: 3g

Chapter 8
Savory Mug Cakes for Quick Meals

61.   Cheesy Broccoli Mug Cake:

Ingredients:

- four tablespoonful all-purpose flour
- three tablespoonful milk
- two tablespoonful shredded cheddar cheese
- two tablespoonful finely chopped broccoli
- one-fourth teaspoonful baking powder
- one-fourth teaspoonful garlic powder
- Salt and pepper to taste

Instructions:

1. In a microwave-safe mug, whisk together the flour, milk, cheddar cheese, broccoli, baking powder, garlic powder, salt, and pepper until well combined.
2. Microwave on high for One and a half-two minutes until the cake is set.
3. Let it cool for a minute before serving.

Duration: One and a half-two minutes

Nutrients per portion (Approximate):

- Caloric content: 260
- Amino content: 10g
- Carb content: 32g
- Fatty acid: 10g
- Fiber content: 2g

62. Spinach and Feta Mug Cake:

Ingredients:

- four tablespoonful all-purpose flour
- three tablespoonful milk
- two tablespoonful crumbled feta cheese
- two tablespoonful finely chopped spinach
- one-fourth teaspoonful baking powder
- one-fourth teaspoonful dried oregano
- Salt and pepper to taste

Instructions:

1. In a microwave-safe mug, whisk together the flour, milk, feta cheese, spinach, baking powder, dried oregano, salt, and pepper until well combined.
2. Microwave on high for One and a half-two minutes until the cake is set.
3. Let it cool for a minute before serving.

Duration: One and a half-two minutes

Nutrients per portion (Approximate):

- Caloric content: 250
- Amino content: 9g
- Carb content: 31g
- Fatty acid: 9g
- Fiber content: 2g

63. Loaded Baked Potato Mug Cake:

Ingredients:

- four tablespoonful all-purpose flour
- three tablespoonful milk
- two tablespoonful shredded cheddar cheese
- one tablespoonful crumbled bacon
- one tablespoonful chopped scallions
- one-fourth teaspoonful baking powder
- Salt and pepper to taste
- Sour cream (for topping)

Instructions:

1. In a microwave-safe mug, whisk together the flour, milk, cheddar cheese, bacon, scallions, baking powder, salt, and pepper until well combined.
2. Microwave on high for One and a half-two minutes until the cake is set.
3. Top with a dollop of sour cream before serving.

Duration: One and a half-two minutes

Nutrients per portion (Approximate):

- Caloric content: 300
- Amino content: 12g
- Carb content: 34g
- Fatty acid: 12g
- Fiber content: 2g

64. Mediterranean Mug Cake:

Ingredients:

- four tablespoonful all-purpose flour
- three tablespoonful milk
- two tablespoonful crumbled feta cheese
- one tablespoonful chopped sun-dried tomatoes
- one-fourth teaspoonful baking powder
- one-fourth teaspoonful dried oregano
- Salt and pepper to taste

Instructions:

1. In a microwave-safe mug, whisk together the flour, milk, feta cheese, sun-dried tomatoes, baking powder, dried oregano, salt, and pepper until well combined.
2. Microwave on high for One and a half-two minutes until the cake is set.
3. Let it cool for a minute before serving.

Duration: One and a half-two minutes

Nutrients per portion (Approximate):

- Caloric content: 270
- Amino content: 9g
- Carb content: 34g
- Fatty acid: 10g
- Fiber content: 2g

65. Mexican Fiesta Mug Cake:

Ingredients:

- four tablespoonful all-purpose flour
- three tablespoonful milk
- two tablespoonful shredded cheddar cheese
- one tablespoonful salsa
- one-fourth teaspoonful baking powder
- one-fourth teaspoonful chili powder
- Salt and pepper to taste
- Sour cream and chopped cilantro (for topping)

Instructions:

1. In a microwave-safe mug, whisk together the flour, milk, cheddar cheese, salsa, baking powder, chili powder, salt, and pepper until well combined.
2. Microwave on high for One and a half-two minutes until the cake is set.
3. Top with a dollop of sour cream and chopped cilantro before serving.

Duration: One and a half-two minutes

Nutrients per portion (Approximate):

- Caloric content: 280
- Amino content: 10g
- Carb content: 34g
- Fatty acid: 11g
- Fiber content: 2g

66.   Caprese Mug Cake:

Ingredients:

- four tablespoonful all-purpose flour
- three tablespoonful milk
- two tablespoonful fresh mozzarella cheese, diced
- one tablespoonful cherry tomatoes, halved
- one tablespoonful chopped fresh basil
- one-fourth teaspoonful baking powder
- Salt and pepper to taste
- Balsamic glaze (for drizzling)

Instructions:

1. In a microwave-safe mug, whisk together the flour, milk, mozzarella cheese, cherry tomatoes, fresh basil, baking powder, salt, and pepper until well combined.
2. Microwave on high for One and a half-two minutes until the cake is set.
3. Drizzle with balsamic glaze before serving.

Duration: One and a half-two minutes

Nutrients per portion (Approximate):

- Caloric content: 260
- Amino content: 11g
- Carb content: 30g
- Fatty acid: 11g
- Fiber content: 2g

67.   Garlic and Herb Mug Cake:

Ingredients:

- four tablespoonful all-purpose flour

- three tablespoonful milk
- one tablespoonful grated parmesan cheese
- Half teaspoonful minced garlic
- one-fourth teaspoonful dried basil
- one-fourth teaspoonful dried parsley
- one-fourth teaspoonful dried oregano
- one-fourth teaspoonful baking powder
- Salt and pepper to taste

Instructions:

1. In a microwave-safe mug, whisk together the flour, milk, parmesan cheese, minced garlic, dried basil, dried parsley, dried oregano, baking powder, salt, and pepper until well combined.
2. Microwave on high for One and a half-two minutes until the cake is set.
3. Let it cool for a minute before serving.

Duration: One and a half-two minutes

Nutrients per portion (Approximate):

- Caloric content: 240
- Amino content: 9g
- Carb content: 31g
- Fatty acid: 6g
- Fiber content: 1g

68.   Vegetable and Cheddar Mug Cake:

Ingredients:

- four tablespoonful all-purpose flour
- three tablespoonful milk
- two tablespoonful shredded cheddar cheese
- two tablespoonful finely chopped mixed vegetables (e.g., bell peppers, carrots, peas)
- one-fourth teaspoonful baking powder
- Salt and pepper to taste

Instructions:

1. In a microwave-safe mug, whisk together the flour, milk, cheddar cheese, mixed

vegetables, baking powder, salt, and pepper until well combined.
2. Microwave on high for One and a half-two minutes until the cake is set.
3. Let it cool for a minute before serving.

Duration: One and a half-two minutes

Nutrients per portion (Approximate):

- Caloric content: 280
- Amino content: 10g
- Carb content: 32g
- Fatty acid: 11g
- Fiber content: 2g

69.   Taco-Inspired Mug Cake:

Ingredients:

- four tablespoonsful all-purpose flour
- three tablespoonful milk
- one tablespoonful ground beef, cooked and seasoned with taco seasoning
- one tablespoonful shredded cheddar cheese
- one tablespoonful diced tomatoes
- Half tablespoonful diced red onion
- one-fourth teaspoonful baking powder
- Salt and pepper to taste
- Sour cream and chopped cilantro (for topping)

Instructions:

1. In a microwave-safe mug, whisk together the flour, milk, seasoned ground beef, cheddar cheese, diced tomatoes, diced red onion, baking powder, salt, and pepper until well combined.
2. Microwave on high for One and a half-two minutes until the cake is set.
3. Top with a dollop of sour cream and chopped cilantro before serving.

Duration: One and a half-two minutes

Nutrients per portion (Approximate):

- Caloric content: 310

- Amino content: 12g
- Carb content: 31g
- Fatty acid: 15g
- Fiber content: 2g

70.   Curry and Rice Mug Cake:

Ingredients:

- four tablespoonful all-purpose flour
- three tablespoonful milk
- one tablespoonful cooked rice
- Half tablespoonful curry powder
- Half tablespoonful chopped cooked chicken
- one-fourth teaspoonful baking powder
- Salt and pepper to taste
- Chopped fresh cilantro (for topping)

Instructions:

1. In a microwave-safe mug, whisk together the flour, milk, cooked rice, curry powder, chopped cooked chicken, baking powder, salt, and pepper until well combined.
2. Microwave on high for One and a half-two minutes until the cake is set.
3. Top with chopped fresh cilantro before serving.

Duration: One and a half-two minutes

Nutrients per portion (Approximate):

- Caloric content: 280
- Amino content: 11g
- Carb content: 34g
- Fatty acid: 9g
- Fiber content: 2g

71.   Caprese Mug Cake:

Ingredients:

- four tablespoonful all-purpose flour
- three tablespoonful milk

- two tablespoonful fresh mozzarella cheese, diced
- one tablespoonful cherry tomatoes, halved
- one tablespoonful chopped fresh basil
- one-fourth teaspoonful baking powder
- Salt and pepper to taste
- Balsamic glaze (for drizzling)

Instructions:

1. In a microwave-safe mug, whisk together the flour, milk, mozzarella cheese, cherry tomatoes, fresh basil, baking powder, salt, and pepper until well combined.
2. Microwave on high for One and a half-two minutes until the cake is set.
3. Drizzle with balsamic glaze before serving.

Duration: One and a half-two minutes

Nutrients per portion (Approximate):

- Caloric content: 260
- Amino content: 11g
- Carb content: 30g
- Fatty acid: 11g
- Fiber content: 2g

72.   Mexican Fiesta Mug Cake:

Ingredients:

- four tablespoonful all-purpose flour
- three tablespoonful milk
- two tablespoonful shredded cheddar cheese
- one tablespoonful salsa
- one-fourth teaspoonful baking powder
- one-fourth teaspoonful chili powder
- Salt and pepper to taste
- Sour cream and chopped cilantro (for topping)

Instructions:

1. In a microwave-safe mug, whisk together the flour, milk, cheddar cheese, salsa, baking powder, chili powder, salt, and pepper until well combined.

2. Microwave on high for One and a half-two minutes until the cake is set.
3. Top with a dollop of sour cream and chopped cilantro before serving.

Duration: One and a half-two minutes

Nutrients per portion (Approximate):

- Caloric content: 280
- Amino content: 10g
- Carb content: 34g
- Fatty acid: 11g
- Fiber content: 2g

73.   Garlic and Herb Mug Cake:

Ingredients:

- four tablespoonful all-purpose flour
- three tablespoonful milk
- one tablespoonful grated parmesan cheese
- Half teaspoonful minced garlic
- one-fourth teaspoonful dried basil
- one-fourth teaspoonful dried parsley
- one-fourth teaspoonful dried oregano
- one-fourth teaspoonful baking powder
- Salt and pepper to taste

Instructions:

1. In a microwave-safe mug, whisk together the flour, milk, parmesan cheese, minced garlic, dried basil, dried parsley, dried oregano, baking powder, salt, and pepper until well combined.
2. Microwave on high for One and a half-two minutes until the cake is set.
3. Let it cool for a minute before serving.

Duration: One and a half-two minutes

Nutrients per portion (Approximate):

- Caloric content: 240
- Amino content: 9g

- Carb content: 31g
- Fatty acid: 6g
- Fiber content: 1g

74. Vegetable and Cheddar Mug Cake:

Ingredients:

- four tablespoonful all-purpose flour
- three tablespoonful milk
- two tablespoonful shredded cheddar cheese
- two tablespoonful finely chopped mixed vegetables (e.g., bell peppers, carrots, peas)
- one-fourth teaspoonful baking powder
- Salt and pepper to taste

Instructions:

1. In a microwave-safe mug, whisk together the flour, milk, cheddar cheese, mixed vegetables, baking powder, salt, and pepper until well combined.
2. Microwave on high for One and a half-two minutes until the cake is set.
3. Let it cool for a minute before serving.

Duration: One and a half-two minutes

Nutrients per portion (Approximate):

- Caloric content: 280
- Amino content: 10g
- Carb content: 32g
- Fatty acid: 11g
- Fiber content: 2g

75. Taco-Inspired Mug Cake:

Ingredients:

- four tablespoonful all-purpose flour
- three tablespoonful milk
- one tablespoonful ground beef, cooked and seasoned with taco seasoning
- one tablespoonful shredded cheddar cheese
- one tablespoonful diced tomatoes

- Half tablespoonful diced red onion
- one-fourth teaspoonful baking powder
- Salt and pepper to taste
- Sour cream and chopped cilantro (for topping)

Instructions:

1. In a microwave-safe mug, whisk together the flour, milk, seasoned ground beef, cheddar cheese, diced tomatoes, diced red onion, baking powder, salt, and pepper until well combined.
2. Microwave on high for One and a half-two minutes until the cake is set.
3. Top with a dollop of sour cream and chopped cilantro before serving.

Duration: One and a half-two minutes

Nutrients per portion (Approximate):

- Caloric content: 310
- Amino content: 12g
- Carb content: 31g
- Fatty acid: 15g
- Fiber content: 2g

Conclusion

In the world of culinary delights, where elaborate recipes often take center stage, mug cakes have emerged as a delightful revolution - quick, easy, and endlessly versatile. The journey through the pages of this book has been a delightful exploration of the world of mug cakes, from classic dessert varieties to savory meals that fill your heart and your stomach.

Mug cakes may be single-serving marvels, but their impact is far from small. They bring comfort to the weary, happiness to the sweet-toothed, and a dash of creativity to the kitchen. As we conclude our exploration, it's worth reflecting on some key takeaways from our journey through "Mug Cakes."

First and foremost, we've discovered that mug cakes are a testament to simplicity and efficiency. In a matter of minutes, you can transform basic ingredients into a warm, satisfying treat that can be enjoyed any time of the day. Whether you're a novice cook or a seasoned chef, mug cakes offer a delicious, hassle-free option.

We've also uncovered the art of customization. Mug cakes are your canvas, and you are the artist. By exploring various ingredients and flavors, you can craft the perfect dessert or meal to suit your cravings. From classic chocolate and vanilla to exotic international flavors, the possibilities are endless.

Our journey has taught us that mug cakes aren't just about taste; they're about convenience. In a fast-paced world, these mini-masterpieces allow you to satisfy your culinary desires without the time-consuming preparation and cleanup associated with traditional recipes.

But it's not just about speed – it's about creativity too. Mug cakes provide a platform for experimenting, tweaking, and innovating. They encourage you to think outside the box, mix and match ingredients, and create your personalized dessert experience.

Furthermore, this book has emphasized that mug cakes are not confined to dessert alone. We've ventured into the realm of savory mug cakes, turning everyday ingredients into quick, satisfying meals. These savory creations showcase the incredible flexibility of mug cakes, proving that they are not limited by the boundaries of tradition.

Our exploration has extended beyond the kitchen, diving into the history and evolution of mug cakes. We've learned that these delightful single-serve wonders have a rich history, dating back to a time when convenience and necessity inspired their creation. From their humble beginnings, mug cakes have evolved into a global phenomenon, celebrated for their practicality and innovation.

As we wrap up our journey, it's important to reflect on the invaluable role of mug cakes in our lives. They offer a slice of happiness during a hectic day, a pick-me-up when we need it most, and a canvas for our culinary creativity. Mug cakes have captured the essence of simplicity and personalized enjoyment, making them an indispensable addition to our culinary repertoire.

Whether you're a seasoned home cook or a newcomer to the kitchen, "Mug Cakes" has given you the tools, recipes, and inspiration to embark on your own culinary adventure. As you continue to explore the world of mug cakes, remember that the only limit is your imagination. So, go forth and bake, experiment, savor, and create your own mug cake masterpieces. The world of culinary joy awaits, one mug cake at a time.

Printed in Great Britain
by Amazon

57896795R00057